The BUSINESS of STUDENT AFFAIRS

The BUSINESS of STUDENT AFFAIRS

Fundamental Skills for Student Affairs Professionals

LARRY MONETA

Student Affairs Administrators
in Higher Education

Copyright © 2021 by the National Association of Student Personnel Administrators (NASPA), Inc. All rights reserved.

Published by
NASPA–Student Affairs Administrators in Higher Education
111 K Street, NE
10th Floor
Washington, DC 20002
www.naspa.org

No part of this publication may be reproduced, stored in a retrieval system, or transmitted in any form or by any means, now known or hereafter invented, including electronic, mechanical, photocopying, recording, scanning, information storage and retrieval, or otherwise, except as permitted under Section 107 of the 1976 United States Copyright Act, without the prior written permission of the Publisher.

Additional copies may be purchased by contacting the NASPA publications department at 202-265-7500 or visiting http://bookstore.naspa.org.

NASPA does not discriminate on the basis of race, color, national origin, religion, sex, age, gender identity, gender expression, affectional or sexual orientation, veteran status, or disability in any of its policies, programs, publications, and services.

Library of Congress Cataloging-in-Publication Data
(Prepared by The Donohue Group, Inc.)

Names: Moneta, Larry, author. | NASPA-Student Affairs Administrators in Higher Education, issuing body.
Title: The business of student affairs : fundamental skills for student affairs professionals / Larry Moneta.
Description: Washington, DC : NASPA-Student Affairs Administrators in Higher Education, [2021] | Includes bibliographical references and index.
Identifiers: ISBN 9781948213349 (paperback) | ISBN 9781948213356 (ePub)
Subjects: LCSH: Student affairs services--United States--Administration. | Student affairs services--United States--Finance. | Student affairs administrators--Training of--United States.
Classification: LCC LB2342.92 .M66 2021 (print) | LCC LB2342.92 (ebook) | DDC 378.1/97--dc23
Printed and bound in the United States of America

FIRST EDITION

CONTENTS

Introduction — *vii*

CHAPTER 1	Student Affairs Financing and Budgeting	1
CHAPTER 2	Organizational Design and Models	17
CHAPTER 3	Human Resources	31
CHAPTER 4	Real Estate and Facilities Management	49
CHAPTER 5	Technology	69
CHAPTER 6	Auxiliary and Other Operations	81
CHAPTER 7	Legal Issues and Risk Management	97
CHAPTER 8	Crisis Response and Management	111
CHAPTER 9	Strategic Planning, Assessment, and a Culture of Evidence	121
CHAPTER 10	Communications	135
CHAPTER 11	Student Affairs: An Uncertain Future	145

The Author — *151*

Index — *153*

Introduction

On the morning of August 20, 1973, my wife and I arrived in Bridgeport, Connecticut, to move into Bruel Rennell Residence Hall at the University of Bridgeport where I started my career as a hall director. I know the date quite well; the evening prior, Judy and I were married in Randolph, Massachusetts. Over the next 46 years, I advanced through roles at five other universities, both public and private, spending the final 18 years as the vice president for student affairs at Duke University.

My career path included many conventional elements: The first 20 years or so were spent primarily in housing and residence life work before a shift to broader roles and responsibilities with oversight of an increasingly complex array of student life and auxiliary services departments. Over the course of five decades, I was fortunate to be invited to learn about and take responsibility for broader aspects of college and university management that enabled me to develop expertise in several "businesses" associated with higher education.

At various times, my responsibilities included oversight of campus-owned hotels, comprehensive hospitality and event management, food services and catering functions, campus card operations, student health insurance, cable television and long-distance phone programs (definitely aging myself here), and more. In my various roles, I have managed buildings, money, and people. My first budget at the University of Bridgeport was probably in the hundreds of dollars. When I stepped down at Duke, my budget exceeded $120 million.

Throughout my career, I often sought unique and challenging opportunities partially because I believed authority came with the opportunity and influence to serve students—my primary objective—and to address complicated needs and issues with the resources and the power to make a difference. My management philosophy was based on the premise that if I had responsibility for functions located within a campus building, I wanted to control the operations of that building as well. This was true for residence halls, student centers, health and wellness buildings, and outdoor areas serving student gathering needs.

Fulfillment of this philosophy required literacy and competency in various business functions that allowed me to hold my own in planning and advocacy with senior business and administration officers, legal counsel, auxiliary services experts, and a wide array of institutional partners within and outside the academy.

I share my background not to tout my career achievements (at least not just to tout them), but to make several points in introducing this text, which will focus on the business aspects of student affairs that anyone aspiring to a higher education role should understand. In particular, I focus on career student affairs practitioners in all roles at all levels. I have always considered myself an educator who practices teaching through student engagement predominantly outside the classroom. I was trained to see residence halls, student unions, multicultural and identity centers, dining halls, and playing fields as laboratories in which students learn leadership, social skills, diversity and inclusion, and the full complement of human and student development skills that underpin the field of student affairs. To be honest, I have watched as each new generation of student affairs practitioners demonstrates highly specialized and essential skills in any number of distinct student affairs practices, yet shows declining capacity to oversee budgets, lead organizations, participate in campus long-range planning and facilities development, and make key managerial decisions.

How to Use This Book

This book is intended as a primer on the business-related aspects of student affairs that practitioners should understand. For every topic, a rich body of literature and an array of educational opportunities are available to dig far deeper. My goal is to arm new and seasoned practitioners with enough information to be informed, engaged, and empowered to the extent they prefer and their institutions permit. I certainly hope this book inspires student affairs practitioners and educators to want to learn more, find connectivity between formal and informal learning through the business of higher education, and seek leadership roles that require mastery of the many topics and issues discussed in the chapters ahead.

Chapter 1 begins with a basic but comprehensive focus on money. Where does it come from? How is it accounted for? How do we ensure best stewardship of resources? Chapter 2 offers a review of student affairs organizational design characteristics. Various organizational models are presented and reviewed along with approaches to restructuring organizations. Chapter 3 focuses on people: What are the key human resource issues and challenges faced by student affairs staff? The chapter examines supervisory challenges, managing up in organizations, equity in salary and rewards, and several other critical personnel subjects.

Beginning with Chapter 4, administrative practices and requirements are explored. This chapter provides a review of principles and practices associated with campus facilities. Among the topics discussed are public–private partnerships and capital development budgets.

Chapter 5 focuses on technology and how best to deploy technology within student affairs. Chapter 6 explores various auxiliary services and connect the dots between student affairs, academic affairs, and auxiliary services. Chapter 7 addresses legal issues and risk management, focusing on how student affairs practitioners should work with campus legal counsel, auditors, and risk management staff. Chapter 8 covers various types of partnerships between campus and non-campus entities and frameworks for achieving optimal relationships with various collaborators. Chapter 9 offers thoughts and guidance on best approaches to student affairs strategic planning and assessment, and Chapter 10 focuses on internal and external communications. Finally, in Chapter 11 all of these topics are tied together with a discussion on administrative competencies expected of student affairs leaders and practitioners as well as the need to build a culture of business sensitivity and sensibility in student affairs organizations.

Let me offer the following disclaimers:

- What has been written reflects my best understanding of the various subjects addressed in each chapter. Any errors or omissions are inadvertent, and I would advise anyone planning to take actions based on information cited in this book to obtain verification from pertinent subject experts and legal counsel.
- The contexts for nearly all matters addressed in each chapter are subject to change. Dynamic laws and policies are frequently under review and adjustment. Make sure to have the most recent information regarding any situation in hand before taking action.
- There is a distinction between being informed and being competent. I may know how a chain saw works, but you would not want me anywhere near your trees with one. The information provided in this book has, in my humble estimation, utility for anyone working in student affairs. To be informed is to be prepared. But health practices are best left to qualified and licensed caregivers. Every practitioner and educator should have a basic understanding of institutional, divisional, and departmental budget structures, but only those with explicit financial skills should be in roles overseeing complex and substantive funding models.

COVID-19 Note

As I write this introduction, the coronavirus crisis continues to ravage the United States, and colleges and universities nationwide are struggling to offer in-person classes, virtual learning, or a hybrid of both. Unemployment remains of significant concern, and many wonder if employment levels will return to pre-COVID-19 levels. Many universities have issued hiring freezes, imposed expenditure limitations, and contemplated other drastic actions to limit their financial exposure. Numerous pundits suggest the heyday of American higher education has passed, replaced by a host of novel educational models, alternative credentialing opportunities, and extended options for virtual, hybrid, and in-person education both synchronous and asynchronous. The demise of numerous colleges and universities could become a reality. The availability of vaccines nationwide gives hope that some form of recovery is on the horizon. The potential future impacts of COVID-19 on processes and concepts outlined in this book are unclear and unpredictable. Time will certainly tell.

CHAPTER 1

Student Affairs Financing and Budgeting

If one were to unpack the business aspect of student affairs in U.S. higher education, it seems logical and appropriate to begin with the notion of money. While our aspirations as educators inspire motivation and creativity, access to resources—especially financial resources—fuels the engines of the many enterprises that serve and support institutions and students. This chapter begins by identifying the various sources of money that enable student affairs entities to operate, followed by a presentation of how to develop a student affairs divisional budget as well as capital budgets for major projects. The chapter continues by advocating for alignment between programmatic priorities and budget development and concludes with a discussion on risk mitigation.

Funding Sources

For most institutions, funding is allocated from central institutional resources, including tuition, fees, investment income, gifts, and auxiliary revenues. Many student affairs organizations augment their central allocation by revenue generation at the division or department levels. For example, a career center might charge employers a fee to participate in a career fair or offer naming rights to an interview room in exchange for a donation to the center. Student health centers often derive income from multiple sources: a student health fee, fees for services outside the scope of primary care covered by the campus health fee, insurance reimbursements, internal recharges to other parts of the institution (e.g., customized healthcare for international travel or athletic participation), laboratory testing, and other specialized care.

The full complement of resources available to the student affairs central administration will be determined by a combination of institutional policies, preferences, and opportunities. For example, an overall student affairs budget might include funds derived from the following sources:

- a base allocation of funds from the institution;
- fees collected by student affairs centrally or through a particular department, such as residence hall charges, student health fees, student activities fees, new student orientation fees, and many others;
- investment returns from gift funds held within the institution's investment vehicles may, through institutional policy,

provide a calculated return on investment to the unit that "owns" the funds;
- gift funds donated with the expectation they not be invested but simply expended over the period of time noted in the gift agreement;
- internal recharges to other institutional entities for services rendered to those units; and
- internal recharges to all student affairs departments at various rates for central services provided by the student affairs central administration on behalf of the division.

Budget Breakdown

Let's unpack each financial element for a deeper understanding of meaning and contribution. Some percentage of the student affairs budget will come as a direct allocation from the institution. The amount of and expectations for using those funds will likely be based more on history and past practices than on some distinct formulaic plan. A student affairs organization with extensive auxiliary operations will commonly self-fund its units and activities as much as possible and leave institutional resources for those units without revenue-generating capacity. There is no hard and fast rule for what percentage of a divisional budget should be institutionally allocated. The more self-sustaining an organization can be, the more likely institutional resources, sorely needed for formal academic initiatives, will be limited to cocurricular functions. In times of fiscal austerity, the institutional contribution to student affairs is vulnerable to reduction.

Fees are complicated and sometimes controversial. Many public institutions have complex processes for fee approvals associated with student services, student-related facilities, and other functions students can approve through campuswide referendums. Independent colleges and universities have more latitude to make decisions about fees and fee levels, but institutional policies and preferences generally guide oversight and adjustment of fees. Fee increases may be suppressed by institutional desire to optimize tuition increases directed primarily at academic initiatives. Even within a student affairs organization, fee levels for various functions will be based on short-term and long-range plans. If the institution aspires to build a new student health center and seeks to reset the student health fee at a substantially higher level to absorb future debt service obligations, a decision might be made to limit all other fees within student affairs so, collectively, the student affairs budget plan will not exceed the institution's financial expectations.

Many student affairs organizations have comprehensive fundraising programs and are significantly involved in soliciting gifts from alumni, parents, corporations, and other stakeholders who support the work of student affairs. Gifts come in numerous forms: one-time allocations to be expended over one or more years; gifts to be invested with only investment returns used as funding sources; estate gifts that provide funds to the university only after the donor's death; and many other variations. Gifts from businesses will often come with more stringent expectations as well as institutional oversight. Opportunities for fundraising by student affairs and on behalf of student functions and facilities will vary from institution to institution. Student affairs development may focus predominantly on parent gifts or may access alumni and other institutional benefactors. (See Chapter 7 for information on the risk of such gifts and risk management in general.)

There are many circumstances in which a student affairs organization might be charging other units of the college and university for various services. For example, student affairs might have oversight for all event management functions for the university. Therefore, it would receive payment from entities across campus for audiovisual support, hospitality services (e.g., tents, printing, catering), conference and event registration functions, and credit card payment processing. How much to charge for these services and what excess revenue or profit margin is reasonable will be institution specific, aligned with campuswide policies and subject to market forces associated with each campus.

If external market forces pressure student affairs organizations to be competitive in their pricing structure for services rendered to the campus, determination of internal recharges to student affairs departments can be challenging. Often, campus clients expect significant discounting from market-based pricing, but such discounting may adversely affect revenue generation to cover the cost of the service and projected for broader budgetary purposes. This model is common, though quite distinct, from campus to campus. Fundamentally, many student affairs organizations have developed a financial structure whereby each department is expected to allocate some amount of funds back to the central student affairs administration for services provided by that entity and staff. Examples of centralized functions on behalf of the organization might include:

- management of all information technology functions;
- human resources support, including staff development;
- budgeting, financing, and all related auditing and transactional processing activities;
- legal services; and
- procurement processing.

Many other functions, for which individual units might be expected to make an annual contribution, could be centralized within a student affairs organization. Revenue-generating units, such as housing, dining, student centers, orientation, and athletics, might be "taxed" at a higher rate than non-revenue-generating units within the division. These arrangements are subject to campus and divisional policies, which can be influenced by the financial challenges of any given year.

Student Affairs Budgets

Budgeting processes and systems are generally distinctive to each institution, subject to enterprise-level applications that may be used more commonly by colleges and universities of all sizes and types. In general, student affairs budget development will follow institutional guidelines and technologies. Typical budget designs assign all dollars to an institution-specific model of expenditures, including separate budget lines for every kind of expenditure. A set of expenditure lines will be associated, for example, with personnel costs, further subdivided by a variety of employment categories. These might include:

- full-time exempt staff (salaried staff not entitled to overtime pay),
- full-time, non-exempt staff (hourly paid staff subject to overtime pay per the Fair Labor Standards Act),
- part-time, non-student employees,
- student employees (funded by work-study dollars), and
- student employees (not work-study funded).

For every category of employee, an institution has its own salary and benefits guidelines and budgetary models. Personnel budgets include projected base pay amounts, anticipated overtime costs, and benefits expenses. Benefit plans are somewhat unique to each institution and may be budgeted as a fixed amount per capita or as a percentage of anticipated payroll expense. Adding to the complexity of personnel budgets may be cohorts of employees who are subject to bargaining agreements (unions) for which pay and benefit structures could be different for each union contract. For each employee, budgets may also include projected expenditure lines for staff development (e.g., conferences and meetings), furniture and furnishings, technology tools, and related items.

The majority of the budget consists of expenditure categories associated with the operations of each unit. For complex and large operations (e.g., housing and residence life or a student health center), the budget consists of hundreds of expense categories, ranging from the plethora of annual facility operations expenditures to debt service payments for capital projects. Programmatic budgets for all units include distinctive expenditure categories for office supplies and equipment, food for programs and events, and the cost of speakers for training activities. Mastering an institution's budgetary model can be daunting, but it is essential to planning and implementing programmatic intentions. Many institutions require a 3- or 5-year budgetary look forward in addition to the formal annual budget submission.

Budget planning is often nearly a year-long process. As a new academic year begins with attention focused on immediate needs and services, department and division leaders must also be engaged in budget planning for the next year and beyond. The budget development process for a student affairs organization is guided by broad institutional as well as divisional expectations and processes. Systems for budget development can be simply incremental (How do you intend to reallocate what you had last year? Where do you need more money? Why do you need more money?) or zero based (Assume no previous budget. What do you need and in what budget categories? Why do you need those funds?). Zero-based budgeting is often reserved for periods of financial challenge when difficult decisions must be made about funding reductions and re-establishment of institution and division priorities.

Capital Projects

Budget development for major renovations and construction projects has its own life cycle and planning process. The student affairs role in capital projects planning and execution depends on the authority and accountability assigned to the division. For example, at many larger institutions, the responsibility for operating and planning campus housing may be assigned to student affairs. That means having accountability for establishing residence hall rates, projecting and achieving occupancy objectives, collecting and accounting for all residential revenues (summer conferences, sports camps, and other non-student uses of residence halls), staffing all residence life and housing operations, paying for everything from utilities to building maintenance to institutional charges for services, as well as myriad expense items, notably debt-service for past capital expenditures associated with a campus housing program.

Long-range planning for campus housing includes future enrollment expectations, projected deterioration and aging of all housing facilities, and the financial capacity of the housing organization, student affairs, and the institution to absorb proposed renovations and new construction costs to address institutional residential requirements and expectations. Publicly funded institutions have their own processes for accessing capital funds, which could include funds from the state. Accessing funds at public institutions generally requires significant compliance with institutional and state technical and formal processes. It can also depend on relationship development and lobbying efforts with key decision makers including influential legislators. Alternatively, housing projects may be required to be fully self-supporting, requiring constant fine tuning of rental rates. As mentioned previously, changes to fees often trigger other fiduciary processes that further challenge and complicate the advancement of capital improvements.

Accessing funds for construction or renovation projects differs substantially from campus to campus. At some institutions, all auxiliary revenues are collected and managed centrally with a portion banked for institutionwide capital needs. Student affairs at such institutions may appeal with compelling arguments to central administration for priority consideration for essential projects. When funding of capital projects is decentralized to units expected to self-support such projects, the institution may "lend" capital funds with the expectation of debt repayment with interest over a fixed number of years. Thus, the cost of capital must be factored into long-range facility enhancement needs and projects.

Competing pressures for access to institutional and public funds have encouraged the development of public–private partnerships. Through such programs, institutions leverage campus land values with capital support from commercial developers to accomplish capital projects without the investment of institutional funds.

Alignment of Objectives and Budgets

A fundamental requirement for a functional and effective program budget is alignment between the program's objectives and the allocation of funds within the budget to meet those objectives. This may seem obvious and inevitable; in truth it is among the most daunting challenges organizations face. Optimally, programmatic strategic planning undergirds all financial planning processes. Periodic comprehensive strategic planning in 3- to 5-year increments should provide the overall "playbook" for advancing the institutional and student affairs vision, mission, goals, and objectives. Annual refinements to this plan should enable timely, opportunistic, and responsive adjustments and pivots to these more immediate goals and objectives. Budget developments aligned with and directed toward meeting both short- and long-term intentions optimize the likelihood of accomplishing the broader and lasting expectations outlined in a comprehensive strategic plan. All of this is easier said than done. As noted above, budget development schedules often preclude an analysis of annual accomplishments, expected and unexpected influences and requirements, and other evolving or sudden pressures for adjustments that a student affairs budget officer would want to incorporate into future budget assumptions. Timelines for changes throughout higher education will continue to shorten as technology rapidly advances; alternative models of teaching and learning evolve; partnership opportunities with commercial partners expand; and global crises and opportunities dramatically influence institutional practices and student needs. Strategic planning and corresponding budget development systems may need to follow shorter time frames with 2-year budgets rather than annual budgets. Regardless, student affairs operations—which are often at the forefront of responding to ever-changing individual and community needs, an assortment of student crises, and aging and high-maintenance facilities—will be best served by closer alignment between programmatic planning and the budgetary process with appropriate "course correction" options and processes to permit effective response to what is always expected: the unexpected.

Fiduciary Risk Assessment and Mitigation

Student affairs budget complexities pose unique risks to those responsible for creating and managing departmental and divisional budgets. These risks include:

- unexpected circumstances and crises, both internal and external to the unit;
- unscrupulous employee behavior; and
- poor financial management practices.

Budgets presume some degree of planning and predictability. A well-designed budget thoughtfully allocates resources to expenditure categories associated with services, programs, and support intentions. For example, a career center budget anticipates personnel costs for career counseling and employer relations staff; facilities costs for career fairs; and travel expenses for staff visiting prospective employers, attending conferences, and meeting donor prospects. Budget lines include allocations for office supplies, technologies, and charges to other university entities. In developing a career center's budget, the director and team review expenditure patterns for previous years, consider changes anticipated in the year ahead, and factor in institutionally mandated costs for new salary levels, infrastructure (e.g., rents, utilities), and other internal charges.

But what happens when a sudden, unexpected, and significant expense hits? For example, a housing and residence life budget with long-term planned expenditures for renovations and new construction must now accommodate a mold crisis uncovered in a residence hall. The building must be vacated, and extreme cleaning and expensive replacement of heating, venting, and air conditioning systems is required. Where do funds come from to resolve this crisis? Many housing operations have the luxury of shifting capital funds from one project to another. There may be adverse consequences in making this shift, including the deferral of much-needed improvements to other buildings, but the emergency conditions can be mitigated with such funding flexibility.

However, this is not always the case. Often such a financial crisis requires support from divisional or even central university resources. These funds could come as an emergency allocation from institutional reserves, from institutional insurance programs or products, or from a loan from the institution to be repaid over a fixed number of years. Any repayment requirements must be factored into future budgets and inevitably influence subsequent capital plans.

When a crisis of this kind happens, questions of adequate preparation may be raised. In this example, should housing and residence life have anticipated mechanical failures with appropriate equipment inspections, preventative maintenance, or replacement? Did the unit annually allocate sufficient funds to various reserve "buckets" in anticipation of inevitable mechanical failures? Should the university's central facilities management operation have had more oversight of the residential facilities? Risk mitigation questions may also call into question the organization of student affairs functions. (See Chapter 2 for a discussion of organizational design.)

Another source of fiduciary risk is associated with individual employee behaviors. Unfortunately, even colleges and universities occasionally hire people who inadvertently or deliberately violate institutional expenditure policies and practices. Fiscal failures through incompetency or sloppiness, such as persistent lost receipts, are at best annoying. Deliberate efforts to divert institutional funds for personal gain are not uncommon and clearly are unacceptable. The burden falls to supervisors and budget managers to enact processes that attempt to prevent and uncover expense violations. Fortunately, contemporary expenditure technologies increasingly limit opportunities for fraudulent behaviors, but any manager or supervisor should be wary of situations where cash is used as a means of expenditure.

More common than unscrupulous employee behavior are ineffective financial practices in an organization. In student affairs divisions, students and staff handle copious amounts of cash, relying on unverifiable receipts for reimbursements and other failure-prone processes. There may be institutional reluctance to assign campus debit or credit cards to numerous student organization treasurers or even to their advisors, limiting electronic expense tracking. These practices are rife with failure, but typically at such small amounts that the concern of university auditors is not raised.

Best Practices

In the future, institutions likely will be far more risk averse, far less decentralized, and considerably more focused on cost savings and efficiencies. In the meantime, best practices for a student affairs financial risk mitigation plan includes the following elements:

- Reduce or eliminate the use of cash throughout the division. Student organizations and advisors should not be collecting dues, event fees, or other payments by cash. Where student clubs and organizations are statutorily independent of the college or university, student affairs might be free from oversight and accountability. As role models and advisors to students and their groups, student affairs is not relieved of ethical obligations to advise of best practices.
- Provide regular budgetary training to all levels of staff. Do not presume new employees arrive adequately prepared for their financial responsibilities. Ensure proper use of institutional financial tools, up-to-date familiarity with all expenditure policies and processes, and continued staff development of fiduciary responsibilities and best practices.
- As is often attributed to President Ronald Reagan, "Trust but

verify." Deploy appropriate auditing tools that permit divisional oversight of unit budgets and expenditures. Central budget managers should regularly check patterns of expenditures, look for charges and payments that fall outside of normal ranges, and require necessary and appropriate documentation of all expenses.

- Partner with institutional risk management and internal audit staff to regularly examine departmental fiscal practices and outcomes. Do not wait for the failure that will necessitate external examination of a unit's books and practices. Persistently and regularly stress test each unit's fiscal practices in partnership with campus experts who are trained and equipped to do so.
- Ensure there are appropriate reserve accounts for moderate unexpected expenses and engage in conversations with senior officials about options for more critical needs in advance of a crisis.

Key Takeaways

Effective leadership and management of any student affairs function and, certainly, of a portfolio of operations, require clear understanding of the sources and uses of all available fiscal resources. Money comes into student affairs from a variety of sources: direct allocation from the institution, revenue-generating activities, and gifts and endowments. Fees for various services may very well be the largest component of a student affairs budget. An empowered administrator will know how to align all sources of funds with institutional, divisional, and departmental priorities. Proper accountability for expenditure of funds, debt repayment, building of appropriate reserves, and support for unplanned crises require a multi-year budgeting process and thoughtful projections of enrollment patterns, capital needs, and other key information that enable sound alignment of all sources of revenues and planned expenses.

CHAPTER 2

Organizational Design and Models

No two student affairs organizations are alike. This may be the most important lesson of this chapter. The organizational design and student affairs portfolio for any institution depend on several factors, including:

- history, traditions, and evolving culture;
- governance principles and practices;
- institution type, size, and complexity;
- consequences of past practices and unexpected circumstances; and
- preferences of institution leadership.

This chapter reviews each of these components and their contribution to organizational design as well as various models for orienting units of student services.

The Role of Faculty

At one time, faculty were expected to do much of what student affairs professionals are now asked to do. Faculty served as mentors and advisors, career consultants, and shoulders to lean on during moments of distress. As faculty shed—or were stripped of—these roles and responsibilities, the student affairs profession emerged and specialized to meet the ever-growing needs of college students.

Each college and university adapted in ways unique to its culture, resources, and capabilities. Faculty members at research universities are often so focused on their research they use grant funds to "buy out" their teaching loads to focus full time on their studies. When they teach, some prefer to limit coursework to graduate classes. While most campuses are blessed with research luminaries, who are also excellent undergraduate teachers, that tends to be the exception rather than the norm.

At teaching colleges, faculty may engage and connect more with students outside the classroom. However, research seems to be a growing enterprise at such institutions as well. The need for student affairs practitioners across the spectrum of services and programs focused on students' academic, personal, and career successes has expanded. Many other changes have influenced the development of new roles, functions, and expectations, including dramatically different student demographics, shifts in student needs and expectations with significant emphasis on compliance and risk mitigation, and extension of support functions beyond a traditional-age, undergraduate, residential student body.

Changes in Demographics and Public Expectations

Diversification of student communities across the country—including more students of color; military-connected students; international students; students of varying faiths, sexual orientations, and ages; and students of various financial means—has transformed campus populations for the better. Meeting the needs of students with such diverse characteristics, backgrounds, and requirements has been a daunting challenge for colleges and universities and has dramatically influenced campus administrative structures—most notably within the student affairs profession. Graduate preparation programs for those entering or rising in student affairs have adjusted curricula and professional preparation to ensure graduates understand diverse student needs, can respond to them, and can advocate for essential support and services where they may not exist. As a result, many student affairs organizations have seen substantial expansion of identity and cultural support centers and accompanying resources and staff. Corresponding changes have included the emergence of student clubs and organizations focused on community engagement for members of various identity groups, residence hall communities designed to accommodate related student interests and identities, and expectations of representative role models and identities among staff in health centers, career centers, counseling centers, and more.

Parent and public expectations have also shifted dramatically in recent decades. Until the 1960s, the legal and ethical doctrine of *in loco parentis* drove college and university support models. Acting "in place of the parent," campuses featured rigid rules regarding student behaviors, limited (so administrators thought) access to students of the opposite sex through "parietal" policies, and punishments for infractions with minimal process and little opportunity for students to mount a defense. That approach changed in the 1960s as students became more engaged and active in the social issues of that era. The Vietnam War, concern with the rights of marginalized populations, demands for independence and representation in decision making, and legal challenges stimulated changes in institutional culture and processes. *In loco parentis* was replaced by the notion of students as adults or, at the very least, of emerging adults with the right to privacy, representation, and fair processes.

Ironically, this generation of students—those who led the way in demanding curricula be relevant, who expected to be respected as independent adults, and who paved the way for the demographic changes—is the generation whose efforts restored a modified form of *in loco parentis*. This generation has insisted colleges and universities protect their children from any possible harm; attend to imperfections—as if anyone is truly perfect—through an expansion of personal and academic advising and support programs; and accept the parent or guardian as a student's agent, representative, and advocate.

Simultaneously, the legal landscape of the nation changed, putting hard pressure on institutions to comply with ever-expanding obligations and expectations. From the emergence of the Family Educational Rights and Privacy Act (1974) to the latest iteration of the Higher Education Reauthorization Act (initially enacted in 1965), campuses have struggled to accommodate and be compliant with local, state, and federal laws governing student disabilities, drug and alcohol use, sexual misconduct, mental health needs, privacy of medical records, fire safety, response to behaviors characterized by hate or bias and much, much more. Accusations of staffing bloat targeting college and university administrations rarely acknowledge the basis for many essential positions.

Added to these service and organizational challenges are societal expectations for the care and support of the broad array of students. Graduate and professional students now seek and expect comparable attention and support for themselves and their clubs and organizations. (Recent changes in collective bargaining rights have muddied that landscape.) Students who only engage via various forms of distance learning (e.g., online courses and degrees, extension classes) and historically were thought to be outside of the campus support infrastructure now expect to be served in ways comparable to full-time students living on campus.

These changes have all contributed to an expansion of student affairs functions, roles, and responsibilities across campuses. Student affairs must now feature expertise and capacity to attend to growing physical and mental healthcare needs of students; assorted student behaviors including sexual assault, cheating, and acts of hate and bias; consumption of dangerous and illegal substances; possession and use of weapons; and various acts of violence. Over the years, student conduct handbooks grew from a handful of pages to the complex tombs that seem now to be the norm. The sole dean who doled out sanctions has been replaced by a team of conduct officers directed by volumes of guidelines and advised by an army of lawyers, risk managers, and compliance reviewers. Student health centers are, on many campuses, full mini-hospitals featuring an array of medical, psychological, and psychiatric staff, labs, and treatment facilities.

Public–Private Institutional Distinctions

A distinction between public and private institutions may also influence the role and prestige of student affairs and of student support in general. Public colleges and universities usually have baked into their culture a commitment to the post-graduate success of students. Those institutions have been the leaders in recruiting and admitting diverse populations, creating personal skills development programs, and investing in student well-being. Student affairs established itself as a profession at such institutions, and many of the student affairs, counseling, and higher education graduate programs were established at land-grant universities. This is not to discredit the quality of or commitment to student success at private colleges and universities, but only to acknowledge the different paths and organizational models that have evolved. It is not uncommon to find a far smaller portfolio of functions allocated to a student affairs unit at a private institution with the complement of services and programs assigned elsewhere within the institution.

Higher Education Isomorphism

American colleges and universities are thought to be bastions of entrepreneurialism and creativity. In many aspects of institutional engagement, this may be true. But, as it pertains to management and leadership practices, U.S. colleges and universities can be quite parochial, following organizational models characterized by familiarity, comfort, and historical replication. A college with a long-standing and cherished dean of students may be loath to tamper with that individual. A university less focused on cocurricular student development may feature a fairly lean student support environment characterized by a just-as-lean student affairs organization.

The same parochialism can be found within student affairs practices. As student affairs evolved and morphed into a discrete set of functions including residence life, student activities, health and wellness, student conduct, and more, each function developed its own culture and standards of practice and professional association. Institutional isomorphism, the process by which culture and practices are replicated from one institution to another, has influenced the development of like standards and culture across all colleges and universities. As a result, organizational design; staff competencies, skill sets, and educational backgrounds; and role expectations look quite similar across most institutions, and hiring authorities have a tendency to seek individuals who resemble the existing workforce.

Collectively, all these influences have contributed to a student affairs environment that is more similar than different, albeit never identical and always subject to local conditions. For example, at some institutions, intercollegiate athletics might report to the vice president for student affairs (VPSA), while at others, notably the elite Division I schools, athletics is more commonly a direct report to the president. Admissions and enrollment management functions, once housed within student affairs, are more often led by a vice president with a direct report to the president or the provost. More recently, health and wellness functions, career services, and academic support functions (e.g., tutoring, academic advising, diversity and inclusion programs, disabilities support offices) have been reassigned from student affairs to other parts of the college or university.

Campus Governance Models

Related to institutional history and culture are the formal processes by which the college or university is governed. Some institutions have retained a strong faculty-led culture that insists faculty serve in dominant leadership roles. The VPSAs at such institutions may be drawn from the faculty, although the increasingly complex and comprehensive requirements of student affairs have limited the number of institutions that choose that pathway. At institutions with powerful faculty senates or other such governing bodies or where the chief academic officer (generally the provost or vice president for academic affairs) has considerable operations responsibility and empowerment, faculty may hold various leadership roles, including chairing oversight committees or otherwise influencing student affairs decision making and practices. In many respects, campuses have found ways to re-engage faculty in the cocurricular lives of students, which is more desirable than not. The reintroduction and expansion of roles, such as vice provost for undergraduate education working in partnership with the VPSA, offers positive opportunities for reconnecting the academic and personal development of students. The success of this model depends as much on organizational structure as on the egos and personalities of individuals in these respective roles.

Members of boards of trustees, directors, and regents, or whatever governing board members are called at various colleges and universities, can be quite influential in a campus organizational model. At many institutions, the board of trustees has a committee focused on the work of student affairs, which may be more or less directive about student support priorities. A trustee-level student affairs committee can be very helpful or can be an extraordinary headache to a VPSA. Having a powerful group of people with the ears of senior institutional officers interested in and engaged in the lives of students will generally be a good thing. Navigating a partnership with and the support of trustees is rife with political land mines. Board members at public institutions may be political appointees or elected officials with political leanings at odds with the institution or the student body. Alumni of an institution may have perspectives of the college or university framed by their own experiences—likely from a period of time with a very different campus environment and structure. Relationships with board members can have substantial influence on staffing sizes, models, and expectations.

Campus Administrative Practices and Preferences

Arguably, the role that could most significantly affect the design and empowerment of a student affairs division is the most senior administrative officer of the college or university. This role appears with varying titles and responsibilities, often as the executive vice president for administration or a comparable designation. The key functions assigned to this role are oversight of all institutional fiscal affairs, human resources, facilities management, including new construction and major renovations, and what some institutions refer to as "auxiliary" functions, including the campus bookstore, postal services, parking and transportation, and more. (See Chapter 6 for details on auxiliary services.)

It is important to understand how institutional history and preferences, coupled with operating principles and structures of the senior administrative officer position, can affect student affairs organizational design.

The organizational design for any given college and university usually has not emerged serendipitously. There is a reason why this unit at College A reports to student affairs but does not report to student affairs at College B. The organizational model of the

Student Affairs Organizational Design Options

In the world of housing and residence life, various designs are found across the country. Institutions that prefer all major renovations and construction projects be managed centrally will often find all facilities planning, construction management, and maintenance centralized within the campus facilities management division. At such institutions, student affairs may have responsibility only for the residence life aspect of the housing environment. Alternatively, many larger institutions endorse a model of housing and residence life led by a director (possibly an assistant or associate vice president position) who is charged with operating the campus residential operation as a somewhat independent, self-funding operation. In the former model, revenues from student housing fees and summer conference operations might be collected and administered centrally. The latter model often features localized oversight of all housing and residence life revenues and expenditures, with accountability resting with housing and student affairs leadership.

Bifurcated operations may exist in the oversight of a student union or center on a campus. In some models, the facilities as well as many of the functions located within the union or center fall under institution is derived from decades of past practices, longstanding cultural conditions (the distribution and concentration of authority among various campus leaders), size, resource capacity, ambitions, and periods of crises that require more extreme adjustments to those models.

the auxiliary affairs division of the institution. In other models, the union or center is operated under a comprehensive design with an individual charged with maintaining the facilities, ensuring optimal operations of the agencies and vendors located within the buildings, and supervising all student-related activities and functions.

Healthcare services are distinctive from campus to campus, subject to institutional culture, preferences, and past practices. The presence of an academic medical complex may also influence a student health service on campus. Under some models of healthcare operations, all student-related health services, including facilities, staffing, and fiscal oversight, are housed within student affairs. There are many variations to these models, including having medical staff report to the medical school or center with accompanying faculty titles. Counseling operations may be separated from all other healthcare operations and report directly to student affairs while the remaining functions fall under the medical center or other administrative entity of the institution. In some cases, a campus healthcare operation serves all faculty and staff as well as students. Telehealth services are growing quickly and substantially on college and university campuses, offering another opportunity for redesigned practices and organizational models for student healthcare delivery.

Influences of the Unplanned and Unexpected

The unexpected can influence institutional organizational designs in different ways. An unanticipated crisis might be limited to the behavior of an individual through negligence or intentional malfeasance. On other occasions, an unexpected crisis could be facility-related, such as the discovery of mold in a residence hall, a damaging fire in a key building, or loss of a major campus utility system. Crises of extreme magnitude, such as Hurricane Katrina on Louisiana campuses or the COVID-19 pandemic, can have devastating consequences. College and university leaders respond differently to such circumstances. Some opt for retaining the familiar campus operations, and others, preferring not to waste a good crisis, leverage the situation to accomplish changes thought to be impossible prior to the crisis. Sudden changes in operating models and conditions can be traumatic to the leadership, often resulting in a cascading set of staff and systems adjustments.

Institutional organizational change is often more evolutionary than revolutionary with occasional spikes stimulated by a new person in a senior leadership role or by a lesser challenge. It is not uncommon for an institution to wait for the retirement of an individual in a key role rather than move expeditiously, often delaying much needed program and organizational improvements.

Higher education is unique in its operating practices. Managerial practices are heavily influenced by people, culture, and environment, and conventional business practices are often secondary to the tenor and timing of the community and relationships. This reflects both the strengths and weaknesses of colleges and universities: Culture and people often trump processes and outcomes.

For someone in a new role at any level in a student affairs organization, it is important to understand the history and the culture that has influenced the design of that operational model. It is also important to remain flexible with that model as administrative structures are always subject to change. The hard part is realizing those changes may come when one least expects.

Key Takeaways

No two colleges or universities feature identical organizational structures. The emergence of the organizational model on any campus is influenced by the history and culture of that institution, by those in leadership and other influential roles, and by stimuli for change, which may include unexpected but opportunistic crises and other unforeseen circumstances. Enlightened and empowered VPSAs understand the historical backdrop to the organizational design in place upon their arrival and leverage institutional governance influences, the development of critical relationships among decision makers and influencers, and peer institutional best practices. They can use this knowledge to advance changes in the organizational model to best meet campus needs, institutional preferences, and strategic objectives.

CHAPTER 3

Human Resources

Throughout this book, a key principle is highlighted that is critical to the success of most organizations, especially student affairs: It's all about the people. As a senior leader, I realized on a daily basis my work was far less meaningful to students' lives and others we served than the work of other individuals in the organizational hierarchy. Every counselor, student club advisor, hall director, audio-visual technician, nurse, and employer relations coordinator served in a far more critical role in direct service delivery. The strengths and weaknesses of all staff members, at every level, determine the success or failure of organizations—especially organizations as human relations and development intensive as student affairs. The need to be aware of and attentive to human resources is essential.

In this chapter, we discuss several key influences on employee performance and production. The literature on human resources is abundant; the focus in this chapter is on the student affairs perspective as it pertains to:

- managing diverse staffs performing distinctive functions in dynamic circumstances;
- ensuring equity in pay and other rewards;
- performance review in the various student affairs professions and divisions;
- professional development, continuous learning, and cross-training;
- negotiating salaries and benefits across employment levels;
- displacing a poor-performing staff member; and
- leadership identification and promotion.

Student affairs organizations are only as good as the people who daily provide student support, services, and guidance. Although intersectionality as an intellectual topic has been discussed for a number of years, it is relatively new to practitioners who focus on diversity and inclusion. Thus, the first imperative for all who touch student lives is to learn more about intersectionality and how its principles can be applied to educational and interventional efforts.

Intersectionality in Student Affairs

In a 2017 publication on intersectionality in higher education, I attempted to address the means by which someone with a host of privileges working in a student affairs leadership role should incorporate the tenets of intersectionality in their work. Student affairs divisions, more than most other college or university organizations, are comprised of diverse staff who represent a host of distinct and blended identities. This is one of the key strengths of practitioner–educator communities that enables us to serve students and others with authentic and empathetic consideration of their needs.

Still, student affairs practitioners face considerable challenges in optimizing supervision and deployment of these diverse employees. The deleterious effects and consequences of implicit biases have been well exposed and explored and require persistent reflection and prevention by those with responsibility for supervising others. Generational differences further confound supervisor–employee relationships such as when a seasoned baby boomer seeks to direct the work of a Generation Z, entry-level staff member. Again, a plethora of studies and findings help inform student affairs capabilities. Suffice it to say anyone working in a student affairs setting would be best served by learning and honing these principles and practices.

Another distinguishing characteristic of student affairs on most campuses is the wide array of functions assigned to and performed by these diverse practitioners-educators. The work of student affairs spans professional practices from event management to healthcare; from career development to food services; and from recreation to information technology. Each practice within the division has its own professional standards, skill sets, and identities. A student union director may feel as much a part of a student union director community around the world than as part of a campus student affairs operation. Counseling center directors have their own professional associations as do staff in recreation, student health, residence life, and other areas. Respect for the work of every student affairs practitioner requires appreciation for the personal history, culture, traits, professional domains, and communities each person brings to the department and the division.

The dynamic nature of student affairs work also affects how vice presidents for student affairs supervise and support employees. In recent years, campuses have responded to pandemics, hurricanes, fires, and floods and to occasions of violence, social injustices, and protest movements. Student affairs often serves as the frontline for such circumstances and young staff, in particular, often bear the brunt of student consequences and anguish. The unique nature of student affairs work requires competencies that span the predictable and the disruptive. Disruption is quickly becoming the norm on university and college campuses globally, placing further pressures on staff, especially entry-level employees, to implement the functions outlined in their job descriptions and adjust to unexpected and quite precarious circumstances that call for responsibilities and behaviors beyond original job descriptions.

Ensuring Equity in Pay and Other Rewards

In nearly 5 decades of work in higher education, I have yet to meet a student affairs colleague whose personal employment goal was wealth attainment. In fact, for many years, entry-level jobs in student affairs paid woefully inadequate salaries. Recent changes to various employment regulations, such as the Fair Labor Standards Act, have helped level the field for salaries and benefits, although many campuses have responded with increased part-time staff and other cost-cutting actions.

The relationship between pay and performance has long been studied, and, for the most part, the literature suggests a limited connection between the two. Particularly in fields like student affairs, salary levels are only modestly linked to work satisfaction, motivation, and performance. For many years, the work of student affairs, comparable to fields such as nursing, teaching, and clergy, was considered a calling—noble, even spiritual work, on behalf of the human condition.

Whether the notion of student affairs work as a calling persists is arguable, but regardless of the level of commitment new staff feel to the profession, there is a greater expectation of reasonable pay, reasonable working conditions, and reasonable balance between work and personal lives. Salaries and benefits may be trending in the right direction, but absent rigorous and persistent review of salary equity among staff, inequities are likely. Remedies for such pay inequities may be challenging where resources are limited or institutional salary scales limit opportunities for adjustment, but to ignore such inequities is unjust, unfair, and perpetuates longstanding biases and imbalances.

Balancing work and personal lives has historically been a challenge for student affairs professionals. Student needs are expanding in type and frequency. Student activities and events are increasingly complicated by legal, fiscal, and operational requirements. The already lengthy outstretched arm of the campus extends even further to worldwide locations. Where more staff is needed to meet expanding needs, colleges and universities are more likely to explore options for retrenchment and labor efficiencies.

For other work conditions, many colleges and universities have led the way in providing various benefits such as inclusive parental leave, tuition support for advanced degrees, and considerable professional development options. Institutional generosity varies substantially, and many young staff have burdensome work expectations, limited support for families and continuous learning, and substandard salaries. In my experience, student affairs leaders who seek to alter the salaries and benefits landscape can be successful by providing compelling arguments supported by incontrovertible evidence. That evidence should include salary comparison studies with peer institutions, staff satisfaction and productivity analyses, and thoughtful and equally compelling strategic plans that showcase the value-added that comes with reforms in working conditions and compensation.

Absent of or in addition to these tangible rewards, many student affairs divisions have introduced recognition and award rituals and ceremonies to honor staff achievements, build staff community and loyalty, and celebrate individual and team talents and distinctions. Examples include achievement award ceremonies, talent shows, and an assortment of social gatherings (food is always appreciated), athletic competitions, and various well-being activities.

The bottom line is student affairs leaders face growing pressures from staff at all levels, especially new professionals, to foster a work environment conducive to contemporary expectations of compensation, work conditions, and personal life. These requirements are likely to be more pronounced in the years ahead.

Performance Reviews in Student Affairs

Everyone is entitled to regular review and feedback about how they are doing in their jobs. Unfortunately, based on years of work in student affairs, my observation is too few supervisors know how to evaluate performance or have the skills to communicate and, where necessary, correct employee performances. From my observations working on several campuses, this problem is not limited to student affairs. I will make an educated guess that it is not limited to higher education.

In full disclosure, I cannot claim to have been the exemplar with regard to performance review documentation, especially with senior-level direct reports. But there are several principles and practices that enabled my supervisees to know where they stood and what they needed to do to correct performance flaws and to excel in their work.

While many of these processes hold true in any organization, they are of particular concern in a profession such as student affairs, which is engaged in human services for the people it serves and the people it employs. Criticism of student affairs work is often tempered by counter-balancing affirmation—meaning that rose-colored glasses prevent student affairs practitioners from seeing and accepting the flaws in student affairs work and the work of others. At its worst, student affairs professionals have a tendency to emphasize the latter and minimize the former, often at professional peril. Employees are entitled to know where they stand and how they are performing in their work individually and as members of work teams.

Professional Development, Continuous Learning, and Cross-Training

In the previous section, the financial investments student affairs makes in staff members and the need to adequately recognize and reward performance was addressed. This section focuses on the further responsibility student affairs has to invest in employee achievement, irrespective of work outcomes. It seems obvious that a profession such as student affairs would want to promote continuous learning and provide as many opportunities as possible for individuals to grow and learn both as employees and, simply, as people. Ample literature on this topic showcases the value of personal and professional development through the workplace.

Principles and Practices for Performance Review

Do not privately horde criticism throughout the year and then dump it on a staff member at one meeting devoted to the performance review. I always promised my staff they would never hear anything for the first time at the performance review session. In fact, I believed the primary purpose of the formal performance review was to meet institutional obligations, and performance feedback should be part of every one-on-one conversation.

When dealing with a performance concern by a staff member, consider whether that staff member really had an opportunity to be successful. Performance problems are often the fault of the supervisor or the organization, which placed the person in a position for which they were actually unprepared or unfit or failed to provide adequate training, supervision, or feedback.

Do not let performance concerns linger. I have seen far too many workaround solutions, most of which have led to staff resentment, dysfunctional teams, and spiraling discontent and disengagement. It is essential that performance flaws be confronted and corrected as soon as possible. Early attention to performance concerns can mitigate far more damaging circumstances and help the staff

Student affairs is fortunate to have many professional associations associated with nearly every aspect of its work. Organizations such as NASPA–Student Affairs Administrators in Higher Education enable those individuals aspiring to broader and more comprehensive responsibilities to connect and engage while simultaneously supporting the full spectrum of student affairs research and practice. Collectively, staff have access to an array of research, online

member succeed. That should be the management focus—helping poor-performing individuals get back on track. All too often, problem avoidance prevails and, like an unattended toothache, inevitably leads to a far more complicated and painful outcome.

Use all the tools available to support staff effectiveness. These tools include the burgeoning business of coaching, 360-degree reviews, personal assistance programs, and reassignment to roles better aligned with the employee's or supervisor's skill set.

When dealing with a performance problem, document everything. There will be an occasion, and possibly more, when someone will need to be displaced involuntarily from their job. It will be painful for the employee and for the supervisor, but inevitably better for both the individual and the organization. Absent an accurate and consistent documentation trail of efforts to identify and help correct performance flaws, institutional policies may rightly prevent a termination or reassignment. I have seen too many situations where documentation of performance failed to acknowledge legitimate concerns because of the supervisor's discomfort in confronting the employee.

and in-person training sessions, and various conferences and conventions. The only things required to take full advantage of these opportunities are encouragement and resources from supervisors and interest and willingness from staff members.

A commitment to continuous learning extends beyond regional and national conferences and programs offered by professional associations. This commitment is not limited to exempt staff and should be reflected by learning opportunities extended to administrative assistants, technical support staff, and others within the student affairs non-exempt community. Fortunately, many colleges and universities provide institutionwide, continuous learning options, including training programs and tuition support for further degree attainment. Many student affairs divisions are fortunate to offer staff development programs, which augment what is available on campus and from other associations. Encouragement and resources are often enough to incentivize employees to participate in these opportunities.

To what end, one might ask, is the value of continuous learning? One response might be: The employee can excel at their work assignment. That response is limited in several respects. It suggests the supervisor's interest is only on the employee's immediate responsibilities, is focused predominantly on the needs of the organization, and is tactical rather than strategic. A better answer would be: Enable the employee to strengthen skills currently deployed, explore interests and capabilities that might lead to new opportunities, and be confident, competent, and able to excel in whatever personal and professional roles and responsibilities come next. Continuous learning is an investment in an individual with dividends simultaneously to the person and the organization.

Continuous learning recognizes the symbiotic relationship between individual growth and organizational progress. As student affairs staff learn, grow, and develop, their students, other clients, and the organization benefit. It means people move up and on, pave the way for next generations of learners–practitioners, and inspire the organization to exceed its own capabilities and expectations.

Student affairs as a profession and a set of practices features many distinctive attributes. As described earlier, the work of student affairs includes a wide array of educational and administrative functions. Student affairs staff members serve as faculty in the classroom and as educators outside the classroom through teaching, training, and mentoring engagements. In many respects, the work of student affairs reflects creativity and innovation. But, in many other respects, student affairs organizations and leaders resist change. As noted in Chapter 2, student affairs divisions are commonly aligned, and members of a particular practice within student affairs tend to seek staff with like backgrounds, experiences, and aspirations. There are benefits to maintaining consistent, professional practices with distinctive standards and like-minded staff just as there are benefits to divergence, differences, and the outsider's perspective.

The development of staff in student affairs should include exposure to the full spectrum of services, roles, and responsibilities across the division and throughout the institution. In my experience, those with the broadest understanding of higher education and its challenges and opportunities, coupled with expertise in chosen practices, develop into the most competent and effective leaders. Staff development programs, which aspire to promote continuous learning and optimization of individual growth and advancement, will offer opportunities to learn and practice the comprehensive work of student affairs and higher education.

There are many ways a staff development program can achieve these goals. In addition to formal skills development options noted earlier, offerings could include collateral assignments to another unit within the division (requiring some release time from current responsibilities); temporary reassignment on a full-time basis to another department; membership on committees and task forces with responsibility outside of the immediate work domain; collaborative presentations at conferences or other training programs with colleagues outside the unit, the division, or even the institution; and support for advanced degrees, research projects, or publications.

Excellence in staff development often means preparing people to do their best work elsewhere. That is, when we enable individuals to be their best selves—to be confident, competent, and capable—we empower them to move on to more influential roles. Those roles may not necessarily be within the current student affairs organization or at the current institution. A commitment to the community of educators and practitioners means student affairs takes great pride in staff achievements wherever they are accomplished. On balance, one would hope that investment would be reciprocated, and employees and campuses would be the beneficiaries of another institution's similar commitment.

Leadership Identification and Promotion

Key responsibilities for management in any organization are to identify and develop talented individuals who, given the opportunity, may rise to positions of leadership and authority. In a student affairs setting, fulfilling this expectation can be fraught with challenges and complexities. First, the process of talent identification can be confounded with various biases and unfair preferences. Implicit and explicit biases in hiring practices adversely affect opportunities for promotion in all organizations. Student affairs, a field dedicated to the advancement of under-represented and minority interests, is not immune from common prejudices in the ways employees are supported and promoted. Student affairs organizations have an added responsibility and burden to ensure equity in advancement opportunities. To do so requires commitments to several types of initiatives: effective staff development and training; regular and persistent analysis of staffing equity in backgrounds, competencies, experiences, education, and salaries; and formalization of talent identification processes to discover new talent and ensure equal opportunity.

As noted, the parochial nature of the distinct practices of student affairs tends to favor people already engaged in the work of that unit despite the potential to recruit better or differently skilled and motivated personnel outside of the unit. Another challenge to student affairs organizations is to balance hiring from within the institution with hiring from outside the college or university. In my experience, a strong student affairs organization is one that embraces advancement from within and outside the institution. Hiring from within the organization sends the message that opportunities for career advancement are possible and desirable. External hiring complements that message by signaling the value of staff diversity, fresh ideas, alternative perspectives, and new and different approaches to student affairs work.

In many cases, problems with poor-performing employees may

reflect a misalignment by management, placing individuals in roles for which they may not have been suited. This issue bears further commentary. The process of recruitment and hiring is part art and part science. The development of a viable and applicable job description grounded in the organization's structural design, aligned with the departmental and divisional student affairs strategic plans, and consistent with parallel and complementary roles, addresses some of the "scientific" aspects of the hiring process. The "artistic" component of recruitment and hiring is often expressed in the exploration of a candidate's fit, particularly for leadership roles. What defines fit? Certainly, alignment must exist between the roles and responsibilities detailed in the job description and candidates' documented skills and backgrounds. To be honest, determination of fit, as observed in numerous searches and appointments, is as much subjective as objective.

This subjectivity of the determination of fit results in many hiring pitfalls. It is where biases may infect the processes. It is where a less capable and insecure hiring authority may opt for a weaker candidate, who might be less threatening to the supervisor. It is where the less qualified candidate might be hired to address a diversity requirement, an act perhaps as prejudiced as avoiding hiring someone because of racial or ethnic differences.

The mitigation of artistic imperfections requires individual and institutional awareness and intervention. Anyone with the authority to hire must be attentive to the possibility of flawed judgment. Any organization must build in processes to ensure fairness and offset these imperfections. Best practices include the establishment of diverse search committees with diversity reflected by identity and organizational perspective; broad and inclusive recruitment efforts to uncover and encourage a broad array of applicants; and an obligation imposed "from above" on every hiring manager to thoroughly document the justification for any particular hiring decision.

Individual Pathways to Leadership

This chapter has addressed leadership identification and hiring from the perspective of the organization and the hiring authority. What about the individual staff member? What can someone who aspires to a leadership role do to be recognized and considered when the opportunity arises?

The pathways to leadership attainment are as diverse as the individuals who seek them. Some people, notably those who tend to be extroverted, may be more quickly noticed. Others may be equally dedicated to their work but less visible to supervisors and colleagues outside their locus of work. This is one reason for an extensive focus on formal and fair performance review processes, which level the playing field for those whose styles and personalities limit their exposure and recognition. Rising stars are everywhere, and an effective performance review process coupled with an equally effective rewards and recognition program helps ensure equal opportunity for their discovery.

No matter what an individual's level of comfort in promoting themselves, there are practices that can help staff with exposure, attention, and consideration for promotion. At the very least, one can and should take advantage of staff development options and opportunities as described previously. Doing so certainly empowers and equips the individual with further skills, and participation in such options alerts management of ambitious and eager-to-learn employees. Volunteering for committees, task forces, and short-term projects or programs offers comparable benefits, as does taking the lead with conference presentation submissions, recruitment opportunities, and search committees.

At some point, one might consider additional formal study in pursuit of an advanced degree or certificate. The decision to enroll in a doctoral program or an advanced degree program in law or business is a complicated one. One must consider whether to study full or part time; to pursue a faster, but more demanding executive degree; to enroll in a conventional program; and how to manage family implications, the cost of attendance, and more. There are rarely easy answers to these questions but, depending on one's academic and administrative objectives, the reconciliation of these issues with the desire to pursue further studies may one day align.

Job promotion within an organization begins with self-promotion. We often think of self-promotion with a bad taste in our mouths: ego driven and more ethnocentric than allocentric. When done correctly, self-promotion is reasonable and necessary. Appropriate self-promotion does not require an individual's success at the expense of someone else's failure. Positive self-promotion enables others to see the authentic values and skills an individual brings to a role and organization. Effective self-promotion may be assertive or passive, loud or quiet, formal or informal, frequent or occasional. The process of self-promotion is highly personal, but it can expose others, especially those in leadership roles, to one's strengths, virtues, and capabilities.

Key Takeaways

The work of any student affairs division is only as good as the work of each staff member. Optimizing individual efforts requires focused attention to equity and fairness in the treatment of staff members; appropriate and effective rewards and recognition processes; encouragement and availability of personal and professional development opportunities; and a culture that supports risk-taking, self-promotion; and course correction when staff or supervisory assignments go awry. Organizations that practice these principles and embrace the concept of individual development as paramount to organizational effectiveness are more likely to inspire excellence in performance and success in serving today's diverse and challenging higher education environments.

Reference

Moneta, L. (2017). Intersectionality in student affairs: Perspective from a senior student affairs officer. In C. L. Wijeyesinghe (Ed.), *Enacting intersectionality in student affairs* (New Directions for Student Services, No. 157, pp. 69–79). Jossey-Bass.

CHAPTER 4

Real Estate and Facilities Management

The work of student affairs takes place on college and university campuses throughout the world. Student and campus community needs are served in residence halls, student centers, recreation facilities, health centers, and cultural centers. Student affairs services also follow students when they study abroad, when they head home for breaks, when they engage in nearby or distant community service projects, and everywhere in between.

Most student affairs work occurs on the physical campus in an assortment of facilities, grounds, and fields for students who attend 4-year residential colleges and universities and community colleges. As online learning models expand, the work of student affairs will inevitably include alternative forms of synchronous and asynchronous support. For example, telehealth pre-orientation, and virtual training programs are increasingly offered. Still, the physical campus and the unique role the campus plays in serving and supporting students remain central to the work of student affairs.

In this chapter, the management of student affairs facilities and the principles and practices pertinent to this work are explored. The chapter covers different operating models, public–private partnership options for both construction and maintenance of facilities, and emerging issues that may alter the landscape of student affairs facilities.

Campus Master Planning

Campus master planning and the master planning of the student-centered environment is essential and extraordinarily challenging. Campuses are always in motion so master plans need to offer sufficient structure and flexibility to guide both lasting campus environments and systems while allowing for evolutionary and, occasionally, revolutionary changes.

Effective master planning, focused on the student experience, begins with a broad reflection of the campus layout: Where are student residences in relation to the major campus academic and cocurricular facilities? Is there a logic to how student-centric environments are laid out relative to desired student encounters, experiences, and services? Are there sufficient community gathering spaces, both indoors and outdoors, hardscape and grassy, designed for specialty uses (e.g., sports fields and performance amphitheaters) and for just hanging out? How does one envision successful "place-making" that is unique to the mission of the institution but allows for flexible, organic growth as well?

It is important student affairs staff understand the physical assets of their campuses, including the conditions of the facilities, community use patterns, gaps between student and community needs, and the institutional physical capacities to address those gaps. The stronger the student affairs articulation of those needs and the means for achieving them, the better the prospects for advancing those plans when resources and political climate permit.

The extent to which student affairs leadership has the responsibility and authority for oversight of various buildings and grounds varies substantially from campus to campus. In general, the larger the institution, the more likely student affairs will manage a portfolio of campus facilities. In Chapter 1, financial models were presented for operating facilities, such as residence halls, as self-supporting auxiliary operations. Following such models, the residential system is expected to generate sufficient revenues from student housing, summer and off-season utilization of residence halls, and other sources to pay for its operating costs and debt service on capital expenses as well as contribute funds for divisional and possible institutional uses. One can find comparable models for athletics, recreation, and other auxiliary operations such as parking and transportation, campuswide utilities, and areas that generate some form of non-tuition revenue. Under these conditions, operational leaders, such as vice presidents for student affairs (VPSAs), could have oversight for the facilities and the functions that take place within those facilities.

An alternative model for facilities oversight is consolidation of all campus facilities under the direction of a senior facilities operations leader. Following such a model, everything—from daily housekeeping to preventative and responsive maintenance services, project management for renovations and new construction projects, oversight of campus utilities, and grounds maintenance—would be managed by this centralized agency. A hybrid of both models is in place at most campuses. Student affairs, even in a highly centralized model, will likely retain responsibility for daily use of assigned facilities and engage in some advocacy role on behalf of the needs and uses of student-centric facilities.

Environmental Design

The science of person-environment fit fills volumes in the bodies of literature relevant to the work of student affairs. It is a field well worth exploring and should be featured in any student affairs graduate training program. Absent a full review of this literature, several examples, grounded both in the science and the art of campus and student affairs design, reflect my own facilities development experiences.

What we do not know about best practices in campus environmental design dwarfs what we claim to know. This may explain why residence hall designs include traditional, double-loaded corridors, suites and apartments, and every imaginable combination of both. It may also explain why the familiar design often trumps the creative, reflected in a variety of student-serving campus facilities.

The design of a building reflects an institution's priorities, resources, and intentions. An elevator placed prominently at a building entrance with stairwells more discretely located in corners might send a different message than an entrance with stairs more visible and elevators tucked away, but appropriately accessible. Ceiling heights, wall colors, lighting quality and options, types of windows and doors, and selection of furniture and furnishings all convey institutional preferences. Seating can be designed to encourage long stays and communal interaction or to promote quick visits and personal privacy. Environments can be intentionally loud and spirited or designed for quiet reflection and calm. Outdoor design can encourage movement or provide options to pause and rest. The role of student affairs in designing a building offers an opportunity to consider what forms of human interaction are desired in a building or neighborhood project and to influence the myriad details that support the desired student and community experience.

Campus architecture is an ongoing battle between form and function. Higher education is fortunate that numerous architects specialize in campus design and, in particular, buildings and environments focused on the student experience. A perennial challenge for campus administrators is to ensure a new or upgraded facility's attractiveness—certainly an essential ingredient—is not achieved at the expense of the facility's functionality. That said, aesthetics matter, and science provides evidence of the positive influences of an aesthetically pleasing environment.

Constructing a New Residence Hall

The process an institution follows to construct a new residence hall is subject to considerable variation. In this discussion, aspects are highlighted that could alter the framework and steps in the process depending on the campus.

Step 1: Developing the Case for Building a New Residence Hall

There are numerous conditions and influences that affect advancement of a proposed new building.

- Long-term analysis of residence hall conditions help clarify the viability of renovation versus replacement. Highly sophisticated and technically capable campus facilities operations, within student affairs or centralized, will regularly produce viable assessments for building conditions. A variety of consulting practices specialize in higher education facilities planning and could be utilized absent such skills at the institution.
- Long-range enrollment plans could suggest the need for more housing capacity or indicate changing market conditions that necessitate a different form or quality of campus housing.
- Access to capital could accelerate investment timelines for new construction. This access could be in the form of state funding in a particular budget year, donor generosity, or financial conditions, such as low-interest loans, that might favor residence hall capital expenditures.
- A crisis condition (e.g., fire, mold, or structural failure)

would necessitate an unplanned or accelerated residence hall replacement project.

Step 2: Developing the Financial Model for the Project Cost

Approaches to financing a new residence hall will differ markedly from campus to campus, reflecting public and private funding distinctions and various financial strategies deployed across higher education. The most common financing approaches follow.

Use of Cash Reserves

The ideal method of funding any new project is simply to have the cash on hand to cover all expenses. In some cases, either through central planning for financial reserve budgets or through comparable planning at the division or unit level (e.g. housing auxiliary budget), institutions have the foresight and capability to build reserve funds expressly for future facility needs. These reserve budgets most often cover a portion of the cost of new construction, but any cash contribution reduces the long-term debt obligation for a capital project. The establishment of cash reserve budgets for new construction or to cover the high costs of maintenance needs is highly recommended.

Though increasingly rare, public institutions in some states can request an allocation of funds from statewide capital funds. Public funds for revenue-generating facilities, such as residence halls and dining commons, can be difficult to obtain given institutional needs for academic and other non-revenue generating facilities. Donor funding is obviously highly desirable, and many institutions have the means to seek philanthropic support from one or more individual or corporate donors to underwrite construction costs. In many cases, recognition options, such as naming the facility for the donor or donors' family, serves as incentive for the gift.

Less common, but worthy of consideration, is the use of commercial contributions from entities that are current or potential commercial partners. This approach is far more common with the construction of athletic and academic facilities, dining halls, and bookstores. Campus and market interest shifts may make this a viable option for new residence halls as well.

Debt-Financed Construction

Debt funding is commonly used to finance residence hall construction. In this approach, the costs of construction, less any cash reserves on hand that can be applied to the project, are borrowed from various sources. Public institutions in some states may borrow funds from a statewide capital "bank," while private institutions generally need to obtain a loan from other sources. Such sources may include an institution's own investment funds, such as its endowment, various commercial lending institutions, or some combination of internal and external lending sources. Regardless of the lending source, generally the expectation is the loan is provided to the institution or the responsible unit of the institution (e.g., student affairs or housing) at an agreed upon or imposed interest rate for a fixed period of time, often 30 years. Not unlike a traditional home mortgage, the debt is expected to be repaid with interest over the term period of the loan. Inevitably, this annual expense is carried within the overall budget for the respective operation.

Public–Private Partnership

A public–private partnership (P3) has increasingly been favored by an array of primarily public institutions with limited access to capital. The need or desire for such an approach may be driven by various campus and state-level rules, including statewide restrictions regarding non-academic construction or institutional preference to apply debt capacity to other campus projects.

A simple version of a P3 could have a private housing developer lease land from a college or university (often at a nominal rate) on which, at the developer's expense, a residence hall is constructed. The private developer receives all or most revenues from the occupants of this residence hall until some date in the distant future when the building reverts to institutional ownership and the formal relationship with the private developer terminates. The benefits of a P3 may be obvious: new construction is completed as needed without using limited institutional resources. The liabilities could include added costs to the project, such as the private partner's profit margin, which will be recovered from the housing fees charged to student residents. In addition, control of design and quality of the facility could be compromised in such a partnership. These are not inevitable outcomes, and many P3 projects have been quite successful in meeting the needs of the institution as well as of the private developer. The key is to anticipate all financial and operational consequences and plan accordingly. For the institution, it is also important to consider the implications of acquiring an aging facility, likely in need of a significant capital investment for rehabilitation, once the P3 is terminated.

Variations to these models differ according to the extent of the private developer's role in administering the residence life program in the building; whether the developer is directly partnering with the institution or, alternatively, with some entity of the institution such as a separately funded foundation; and expectations and limitations agreed upon relative to architectural standards, ongoing maintenance, and occupancy commitments and plans. P3 models abound, and VPSAs seriously considering a P3 approach to new construction would be well advised to thoroughly review the opportunities and consequences of this strategy.

Use of Student Fees

At some institutions, student fees—subject to the outcome of a student referendum—underwrite the debt service associated with a facility such as a student union–center. While the voices of students are important for any campus project that affects them, it is critical that students be involved in this type of decision from the earliest determination of need and intent to garner their support for the referendum-backed funding process.

Step 3: Designing the Residence Hall

Campus housing designs vary substantially, depending on institutional preferences for the residential model and experiences. In establishing the case for a new facility, consideration should be given to what type and size building is desired. Concurrently, preliminary analysis of likely sites and the scope of the project should be completed as part of the project's initiation. The formal design of a building usually requires the services of an architectural firm, preferably one with campus residence hall design expertise. The process for selecting an architect will also vary from campus to campus and might include some form of design competition, deployment only of state-authorized firms, use of a previously selected campus master planning firm, or an open call for design proposals. On many campuses, the selection of an architect is centrally controlled and may require the approval of the president and the board of trustees. The roles and responsibilities of student affairs and the housing unit with architect selection vary by campus and institutional design standards.

Achieving Design Success

Once an architectural firm is selected, the hard work of designing the residence hall begins. The success or failure of the design rests on several elements.

- Architects perform best, based on my many years of involvement with numerous construction projects, when the project is crisply and definitively portrayed. Generally, the design process begins well before the selection of the architect, but often the architectural process will launch with a review of preliminary program plans and a more formal determination of the project details. At the end of this phase, documentation must be produced that denotes precisely what the institution desires when the building is complete: overall layout of the building; number, size, and type of rooms; community gathering spaces; ancillary facilities (e.g., kitchens, workout facilities, laundry rooms); staff apartments; and landscaping preferences. Institutional site and utility requirements, design standards, and code requirements should be incorporated and agreed upon as well.

- A successful program plan guides the architectural design and ensures alignment between form and function. It is also a living document and will be revised regularly as new information influences the design of the building. Cost implications, site conditions, code fulfillment obligations, and stakeholder feedback will inform and influence what is possible, what is affordable, and what is absolutely necessary as the project moves forward. On most campuses, a project management entity—either an internal agency of the institution or a contracted partner—facilitates ongoing discussions and negotiations between the architects and the campus client (e.g., student affairs, housing, or other campus player in charge of this project) as documentation continues to be molded and shaped to balance campus needs with available resources.
- The aesthetic requirements of this project will be influenced by several factors, some previously noted. Many campuses have design standards that direct choices of materials, colors, and shapes. A campus with a single vocabulary for all buildings (e.g., University of Virginia) will obligate the architect to design the residence hall consistent with all other campus buildings. Most campuses invite some measure of design creativity within formal institutional boundaries intended to ensure environmental coherence. In my experience, the best architects test the boundaries of campus design standards with interesting and innovative concepts. Ultimately, the architectural process will yield a functional and attractive building design that satisfies end-user program requirements,

the institution's campus layout preferences, and the financier's wallet.

Step 4: Construction Management

A construction company is hired approximately concurrent with the selection of the architect. Ideally, the construction firm works hand-in-hand with the architect to ensure the viability of the design and to estimate construction costs. Throughout the design phase, the proposed models should be reviewed and critiqued by the construction firm to ensure clarity of intentions and consequences relative to constructability. As the costs associated with meeting design requirements evolve, adjustments (*value engineering* is the term often used to denote elimination of various project elements in order to achieve expense reductions) will inevitably be made to the design to meet budget limitations. Managing these critical negotiations to ensure alignment between program requirements, design preferences, and financial expectations is a challenging process often led by the campus construction project management unit or a consulting practice engaged to perform this function on behalf of the college or university.

Construction Considerations

There are several principles and practices to be aware of when engaging in any construction or major renovation project. The unique nuances of every project assures considerable variance in the applicability of each principle or practice, but collectively, they provide a useful and realistic template for how best to be prepared for facilities development projects.

- Many players are involved in the construction of a residence hall besides those previously noted. Generally, the contractor (construction company) or architect will engage a team of subcontractors who provide additional expertise and services to the project. Members of this team might include landscape architects to address the grounds surrounding the building; various engineering firms that focus on heating, venting, and air conditioning aspects of the building; and other vendors to address everything from utility systems and fire suppression to technology applications, interior design, appliances, and more. The quality of the final product depends on the expertise of these subcontractors and the level of their collaboration.
- The time between project initiation and groundbreaking may be a year or more. There are numerous and complicated processes that precede construction. Some aspects of the project, such as site preparation (e.g., tree removal, fencing, and redirection of public pathways), can occur as final design and construction plans are completed. The actual initiation of the construction project requires all the steps noted above, compliance with all local permit requirements, and final approval by senior administrators and possibly the board of trustees.
- Once the groundbreaking ceremonies are complete and shovels are in the ground, the urge to make subsequent changes must be resisted. Cost overruns are frequently associated with changes requested by the client. The project management team, whether an internal group or under contract to represent the campus, has responsibility for assuring

compliance with all aspects of the construction contract. The team's job is to minimize unexpected expenses, though some will be inevitable. Unexpected site conditions, adverse weather, labor issues, and accidents do happen, but good planning, good contracts, and good relationships mitigate unplanned and unaffordable exposure.

- Construction of a residence hall often brings ancillary challenges to the campus community. The new residence hall might be built adjacent to existing residences or campus facilities, and this construction will raise issues such as noise, vehicular and pedestrian travel concerns, loss of parking, and a host of other issues. Good planning anticipates many of these concerns and creates solutions to minimize (but never eliminate) the inconveniences.

Depending on the size and complexity of the project, 1 or 2 years after construction has begun the new residence hall will be ready for occupancy. All that remains, besides the use of the building, is annual payment of any project debt.

Other Student-Related Facilities

The construction of any facilities associated with student affairs work could follow a nearly identical sequence. The nature of the various student-focused facilities could alter the planning process or elements, the participants in the processes, and the financial implications.

- A student health facility may require specialty consultants with expertise in medical facilities and operations. If the building is intended to incorporate a full primary care clinic, counseling center, pharmacy, health education unit, physical therapy office, and other health-related service components, each aspect might require unique expertise as well as architectural and construction talent with appropriate experience. The same will be true for a recreation and athletics project, a student union–center, or for any kind of food services facility, all of which require substantial, distinctive expertise.

- Each of these examples requires thoughtful and comprehensive planning to take into consideration market conditions, institutional objectives, financial limitations, operational analysis, and mid-construction community consequences.
- Smaller projects, such as the renovation of a health clinic, the relocation of a cultural center, or an upgrade to a dining facility, are best accomplished with the same discipline. Stakeholder involvement is more critical for some projects than others, with student involvement of more importance in some circumstances.

Much of this chapter has addressed aspects of person-environment fit pertinent to individual facilities and buildings. Of equal and perhaps greater importance is how groups or clusters of facilities and services associated with those facilities might collectively advance student affairs programmatic objectives. The notion of adjacencies has great relevance and impact to student affairs aspirations. A student union–center development project serves as a vivid example.

Student Unions–Centers

No two conceptions of a student union–center are exactly alike. On some campuses, the student union–center serves as the primary student dining hub for the institution, while at another college or university recreation facilities may be co-located within or next to the student union–center. Some facilities feature significant auxiliary presence (e.g., bookstore, bank, conference operations), while others primarily house student activities and leadership development offices, cultural and identity centers, and other student community engagement offices. Finally, some student unions–centers serve as the arts hub of the campus with theaters, galleries, and other performing arts spaces or serve faculty, staff, and alumni in addition to the student population.

Regardless of the campus model for its student union–center, the layout of the building (i.e., where the functions, offices, and facilities are located) conveys messages about institutional priorities and desired outcomes. For example:

- Are offices that serve underrepresented and minority students located in highly visible and accessible locations or relegated to hard-to-find locations?
- Do the locations of various offices and functions promote or inhibit cross-communication and interaction between various student communities that might not otherwise interact?
- Does the building promote good customer service through ease of access to high traffic offices and services?
- Do the public spaces of the building offer thoughtful connectivity to the various offices and functions within the building?

These questions are intended to invite consideration of a thoughtful facility layout that might advance an institution's objectives through the casual and unforced interactions associated with daily passage through the building and the spaces around the building.

Student Precincts or Neighborhoods

The same principles can be applied to a collection of buildings and outdoor spaces that could create an environment where dining, healthcare, student events and activities, student residences, and more can be assembled, aligned, and operated in ways that promote interaction, communication, and cross-pollination of ideas and interests. Campus master planning should generate a long-term, physical conception of the college or university campus that orients various aspects of the campus in a logical, efficient, and symbiotic environment. It offers an institution the opportunity to envision campus development as a set of interconnected elements that place academic, community, residential, and service aspects in locations that optimize the intended functions of the various buildings and collectively knit this collection, and adjacent grounds, into an overall environment of interdependent functionality, beauty, and distinction.

A campus facilities master plan is a living document shaped over time, incorporating institutional priority changes, external and internal influences from all stakeholders, and resource opportunities and limitations. It permits thoughtful consideration of parking, transportation, campus pathways, and other mobility elements. It provides the means to establish relationships with the local community by defining public entrances and service access points. It enables the campus to develop potential construction sites while preserving lands preferred for other uses. For student affairs purposes, an effective facilities master plan delineates housing, dining, recreation and fields, student activities, health and well-being, and various other student- and community-centric facilities and environments. It permits careful consideration of the relationship between and among each of these student-serving elements with an optimal approach to their adjacencies, consequential student movement throughout the campus, and intended and implied messaging about the location of support and service offices.

Key Takeaways

Any student affairs professional aspiring to a VPSA role must become sufficiently familiar with and competent in campus facilities development and operations and must be prepared to advocate for and influence needed renovations and construction. Depending on the size and scope of the student affairs division, embedding facilities oversight talent within the student affairs team—either as a dedicated position, part of several staff roles, or by contract with an appropriate consulting group—could be considered. Ultimately, person–environment fit extends to communities–environment fit, meaning residential communities; communities defined by identities, interests, and cultures; and communities of students, faculty, staff, alumni, and others. By being deliberate and attentive to environmental design and excellence, the potential for excellence in the care and support of an institution's communities is elevated.

CHAPTER 5

Technology

Any discussion on technology runs the risk of being outdated by the time of publication. The pace of technological changes—affecting both hardware and software, apps and platforms, and synchronous and asynchronous components—is fast and accelerating daily. No aspect of student affairs, nor of higher education in general, is or will be untouched by technological influences and applications. In the months and years ahead, one should expect significant further technological advances in the ways students and campus community members are served and supported.

This chapter covers several levels of student affairs technology topics, beginning with principles that can guide student affairs work, followed by an examination of technologies, from enterprise-level to unit-specific applications, and a discussion of mobility, as well as mobile and desktop devices. The chapter ends with thoughts about possible future technologies that could dramatically influence the work of student affairs.

Student Affairs Technological Competencies

It is useful to begin a discussion of technology with thoughts about the level of technological competency expected of student affairs staff. Beyond the obvious use of technology for correspondence and communications and some literacy in developing spreadsheets and surveys, what else should be expected of staff at the various levels of a student affairs organization? A common misconception is that younger and newly hired staff will be more up to date on the latest applications favored by students. In truth, digital fluency varies considerably among student affairs practitioners, and the development of technological competence should be promoted throughout any student affairs operation and prominent within all student affairs and higher education graduate preparation programs. Technological literacy across the spectrum of student affairs functions and processes is essential to any contemporary operation. Staff members—from entry-level positions to vice presidents for student affairs—are exposed to the consequences of technology through every email sent, social media employed, data management platforms and programs used in various student affairs practices, budgets developed and funds expended, physician or counselor meetings with students, program assessments, personnel reviews, and more. Every staff member needs a baseline technology literacy level, and many require more advanced skills development consistent with the technological requirements of their specific roles.

Where can staff obtain relevant and timely technological competencies? Most colleges and universities offer training opportunities; consultants and conferences focused on technology abound. Professional associations, such as NASPA–Student Affairs Administrators in Higher Education and ACPA–College Student

Educators International, offer useful guidance on the promotion and development of technological fluency. All student affairs divisions should build technological advancement and competencies into their staff development programs.

Principles of Technological Competencies

The time between adoption and retirement of an application grows shorter every year. At the moment, Tik Tok is on the rise and Facebook appears on the decline—at least among the traditional college-age population. It seems reasonable those who work directly with students are familiar with application trends and fads. But what principles should govern both the competencies and skills of staff and the appropriate use of technologies? Consider the following principles:

- Knowing how students engage online does not mean staff should participate in an identical manner. Preservation of student privacy is paramount, and casual lurking in student online spaces exposes staff and the institution to considerable risks. (See Chapter 7 for more information on risks and risk management.) Defining proper staff online behavior is difficult to do with precision. Online behaviors that overtly interfere with, expose, or otherwise embarrass or insult others must be avoided.
- The flip side of this coin is the need for student affairs staff to be aware of issues and circumstances of importance to the division or the institution. Good online practices include attentiveness to activities and events that may have some

bearing on the institution; to individual and group communications that may be of threat to the individuals or the community at large; and to local, regional, national, and even international online messaging that could affect the campus and the community.
- Nearly every practice within student affairs has unique applications that apply to those distinct functions. It is reasonable to assume staff will develop prolific competencies on the explicit applications of their distinctive practices.
- Online, group video communications have become commonplace. Prior to the COVID-19 pandemic, the use of group webinars and video conferences was rapidly expanding. Subsequently, their use has grown exponentially, and one would expect this practice to be more universally deployed in the future, necessitating universal competency for staff at all levels.
- Rapid deployment of many other student services to virtual applications, both synchronous and asynchronous, is underway. Skills development in the online use of chatbots, telehealth, wellness, other life skills programming, and transactional services is increasingly essential.

Resources Allocated to Technology

The emphasis and dependency on technology throughout higher education and student affairs necessitate access to expertise and support. Larger student affairs operations may include in-house information technology personnel. At smaller or less resourced institutions, support may be centralized. Support to student affairs will range from simply enabling and maintaining desktop and mobile equipment for each staff member to managing data and data storage and contracting for and licensing numerous applications.

What equipment and applications should a student affairs division provide to each staff member? The response to this question will differ from campus to campus, depending on institutional policies, preferences and resources, as well as the requirements of various roles. Some individuals are in roles and have responsibilities that require far more computing power, memory, and data access privileges than others. Those responsible for budgets and personnel may require different tools and information access consistent with their work requirements. For the majority of the student affairs staff, computing and communications needs will be satisfied with a basic array of equipment, including a desktop or laptop computer and smartphone. As tablets evolve with increasing applicability and computing capacity, some institutions have begun issuing tablets rather than far more expensive laptop computers for staff use. It is not too hard to imagine a smartphone that expands to a tablet as a universal computing tool one day.

Policies and Practices Governing Use of Technologies

Consistent with these principles, student affairs policies should be developed to guide appropriate use of institutionally provided equipment, storage and sharing of data, and safety and security expectations. Optimal device and data management include data backup policies and practices, ideally seamless through a division or institutionwide data backup system. Other appropriate practices include the use of virtual private networks, virus detection and intervention applications, and remote service and location applications.

Cloud storage of data is now commonplace, which relieves the need for local storage on computing devices. The amount of information retained and regularly accessed in a contemporary student affairs operation can be overwhelming and unmanageable. Information overload makes clear the need for effective and efficient data and information management policies and staff to ensure proper organization, accessibility, and use of the enormous trove of data generated daily across multiple platforms and programs within student affairs.

Much of the data accessed with frequency by student affairs operations reside within institutionwide data sets and storage. As centralized student information systems become both commonplace and comprehensive, student affairs practices regularly access these central databases for students' academic and non-academic information. That information may be ported to a local or application-specific database where other pertinent information resides and can be merged for program purposes or for the application in use.

- o Student conduct records may be retained in a student affairs data set and housed in a cloud-based storage application with appropriately limited access privileges. Conversely, these data could be stored by a private, student conduct information management provider in their appropriately secured, proprietary information storage system. In either case, it is likely this conduct management application requires secure access to the institution's student record system to download and supplement conduct data with other relevant institutional

data. In addition, uploading the outcome and consequences of a conduct process to the student's permanent institutional record may be required.
- Medical records maintained in a student health medical records system or case notes from a counseling center's record-keeping program may require comparable connectivity with students' institutional records.
- The same issues are relevant to career center applications (internship and employment support services), student activities (club and organization membership and activity records), and every student affairs department.

What should be obvious at this point: It is critical that information be appropriately and effectively protected. Much of the information described in this chapter is legally protected under the provision of the Family Educational Rights and Privacy Act (FERPA) and under the Health Insurance Portability and Accountability Act (HIPAA) for medical records. All student affairs staff must be familiar with the requirements of these acts, and those with access to any medical records must have detailed knowledge of and training in HIPAA requirements.

Protection of Student Data

Student data are regularly obtained, stored, and utilized. Data come from pre-existing institutional or local databases. With the advent of simplistic survey administration programs, anyone can be a social science researcher. Good management practices in student affairs require evidence of effectiveness of various initiatives and efforts.

That evidence is often derived from assessment and evaluation processes that could include survey research, which has been significantly enabled by the development of user-friendly survey instruments.

In most cases, the deployment of well-developed assessment instruments and the collection of feedback and impact information from students and other student affairs clients are desirable and well regarded. In addition to all the protections described above, any such data collection must comply with a college's or university's institutional review board (IRB) requirements and protocols. An IRB exists at nearly every institution and governs the collection of research data. It ensures appropriate processes for data collection, identity protection for individuals, and alignment of survey approaches with scientific methods for research design, data management, and record keeping. Student affairs staff should be as familiar with IRB expectations as they must be with FERPA and HIPAA.

Third-Party Partnerships and Data Management

Concerns about the protection of information suggest the need for highly informed and professional practices when developing relationships with third-party, private technology providers, especially when data utilization and storage are involved. Such partnerships are common in the areas of conduct, health records, student engagement, and activities, but they are increasingly evident in other student affairs functions from housing room assignments to orientation registration programs. The development of an effective, reliable, and compliant partnership with a technology provider can be optimized with the following steps.

- The process for choosing a technology provider should rarely begin with exploration of any particular application. The first step in considering the adoption of any technological platform should be the development of a set of functional requirements by the unit seeking the use of an application. A functional requirements document offers, in non-technological language, identification of the specific needs of the unit, problems to be addressed, and processes and functions that are intended to be automated. This functional requirements document then becomes the assessment instrument by which all potential applications can be measured for consistency and applicability.
- Broad stakeholder participation is essential to effective identification and adoption of an application. Those with expertise in third-party contract management (often a campus procurement office), information technology security, risk and legal requirements, and cost implications should be included in decision making.
- If the application requires connectivity to other databases, such as the campuswide student record system, validation of information portability, compliance with institutional and legal data management, and agreement on the location and accessibility of data storage are essential.
- Rarely will a third-party technology solution be viable for use without some customization to meet the needs of the acquiring unit. The contractual, negotiated agreement should articulate with clarity the level of customization available to the institution, timing, and costs. The installation and adoption

processes for engaging the product should also be outlined in detail. The better the understanding of what is expected from the institution and the private provider, the more likely a smooth transition and positive relationship.

Financial Implications

The cost of essential and effective technologies for student affairs use will be high. The cost of obtaining and attempting to use wrong or poorly developed technologies will be far higher. The rapidly changing universe of technological tools and applications suggest contract periods should be relatively short with institutions retaining options for terminating agreements relatively quickly—perhaps as short as 30 days.

Future Considerations

What about the future? What technologies should student affairs anticipate that will further transform the nature of the work, the staff, and the institution? Asynchronous and synchronous online teaching, advising, and transactions with students and others are likely to become normative and expansive. Online activities will not adequately substitute for every communication, transaction, and connection between students and staff, but virtual options work better than expected for many student affairs functions and certainly are viable for engaging with students while they are traveling, at home, or ill. Online meetings, especially those involving participants in multiple locations, will likely become more common. Implications of frequent online engagement include the need for absolutely reliable technologies and increased staff competency to effectively deploy the technology. Rules of engagement that curtail poor online behaviors, enable identification of students in distress, and customize online delivery of care and support require further development.

Artificial Intelligence and Robotics

Artificial intelligence (AI) and robotics will disrupt traditional student affairs practices as well. AI-informed practices may render obsolete many frontline functions limited to information dissemination. AI tools will one day pick up on signals of distress, connect students to appropriate responses, and provide solutions. AI tools and various forms of robots will handle housing assignments, resume reviews and interview scheduling, diagnosis of simple medical needs, and various forms of dispute resolution. AI-powered robots already deliver mail and packages and may eventually cook and serve meals in dining halls, as well as clean restrooms and hallways. Autonomous vehicles may roam the campus, providing escort services to keep students safe at night and ride-share functions across and beyond the campus. Add smart toilets, remote sensing, video security platforms, and biometric access features and the residence hall of the future begins to take shape.

Colleges and universities already see exponential growth in e-sports, even as spectatorship rapidly declines at campus stadiums and arenas. Gaming will not be limited to recreation and entertainment, as the gaming industry stimulates healthier personal practices, positive environmental behaviors, and more effective educational techniques. As further advances in behavioral and biological sciences, AI, and robotics emerge and other scientific discoveries evolve, it is difficult to imagine the technological advancements that will alter the work of student affairs.

Key Takeaways

The future of student affairs will involve far more use of and dependency on technology. Transactional relationships will become increasingly automated, and advances in AI will enable machines to perform many basic functions. Certain student affairs services will become a hybrid of technology and human effort, requiring considerably more technological skills development and competencies among practitioners.

Technological training and education must begin with the earliest introduction to the field of student affairs and persist through staff development programs within the institution, professional associations, private partnerships, and more. Technological literacy necessitates the development of best practices that satisfy ethical, legal and the most effective outcomes. Just as a student affairs operation becomes comfortable with its own technological landscape, change is on the horizon.

CHAPTER 6

Auxiliary and Other Operations

The term auxiliary operations is, in many ways, anachronistic. It evolved over many years as colleges and universities expanded operations and services and recognized all academic activities as primary and other back-of-the-house functions as auxiliary. This chapter reviews various programs and services traditionally thought to be auxiliary and offers insight into the relationships between many of these functions and student affairs operations. Alternative approaches to strengthening interrelationships and partnerships between so-called auxiliary services and student affairs are offered.

Origins and Models

In 1969, the National Association of Campus Auxiliary Services was formed to support the work of administrators with responsibility for non-academic functions such as bookstores, parking and transportation, postal and mail services, food services, conference and event management, identification card transaction functions, and more.

The existence of auxiliary services, under alternative names on different campuses, begs the question of how student affairs is defined and where its services and operations fit within any institution. Since student affairs leaders generally report to the president or the provost of the college or university, the argument most often made is that student affairs work aligns most closely with other academic support functions, such as advising, library services, or athletics. In truth, the lines between student affairs, academic affairs, and auxiliary services are quite blurred. On many campuses, food services are overseen by student affairs staff, but career services might be operated by alumni affairs. Conferences and event services are often embedded within a housing or student union–center operation or aligned within a comprehensive hospitality services operation under an auxiliary services division.

In reality, institutional boundaries between various functions are locally derived, governed by the history, traditions, and operating preferences of senior management and subject to opportunistic and serendipitous changes as campus and external influences shift. The fluid nature of these boundaries and the expanding and contracting portfolios of student affairs divisions suggest the need for a better understanding of these practices by student affairs staff. Several operations that span the boundaries between student affairs and auxiliary services offer insights into these challenges.

Food Services

A campus food service operation is fascinating and extraordinarily complex. In many cases, the comprehensive food services operation includes both a formal student dining environment and model in addition to dining venues and operations focused on other campus communities and the public.

Models for student dining abound across colleges and universities. Variations include dedicated venues and systems designed exclusively for first-year students, which may be affiliated with a first-year residential campus or set of residences. At the other end of the spectrum, a comprehensive dining common could be designed to meet the food needs of all students, as well as faculty and staff. Every variation imaginable exists on some campuses. Board models (as in room and board or dining) include all-one-chooses-to-eat designs where students simply swipe their identification card, enter the dining venue, and eat to their hearts' content. Alternatively, a campus might feature a declining balance model with a prepurchased, set amount of points, which are then expended on an *a la carte* basis in designated venues across campus. Hybrid models offering both options are included in student dining plans at some institutions.

Colleges and universities choose dining models based on several factors. Some administrators see the dining environment as very much a part of the student's community development environment and prefer dining models that emphasize "stick" (dining vernacular for time spent at meals), group engagement, and conversation, often populated by nearby residence hall living communities. Those institutions that focus more on customer service, efficient operations, and cost implications might favor grab-and-go models (characterized by prepackaged meals, speedy service, and a high number of clients) to expedite revenue generation and customer preferences. Again, most institutions worry about the context and design of their dining models to optimize the communal experience and meet customer expectations and desires.

Dining operations can be self-operated, contracted, or both. In a fully self-operating model, all campus dining operation staff are college or university employees, all the food venues are owned by the institution, and all revenues (e.g., board plans, retail operations, catering) and expenses are the responsibility of the institution. On various campuses, many dining employees are members of a collective bargaining unit within a union with work rules, salaries, and benefits all subject to periodic negotiations with the institution. Self-operating dining models are responsible for procurement of food and supplies, cleaning and maintenance of dining venues, preparation of all meals, management of payroll and expenses, and coordination and execution of functions from marketing to nutrition advising. All capital expenses in such a model are the responsibility of the college and university, generally funded through net dining revenues.

Many campuses prefer to outsource dining operations to one or more partners. In a fairly common model, an institution contracts all dining operations to a comprehensive food services provider. That provider employs all staff who are part of the dining program, thus relieving the college or university of any responsibility for staffing, acquisition of food, and related operations. Typically, the institution owns the campus facility where the private provider operates the dining venue, which is either leased to the provider or assigned to their use as part of the contract. Often, with fully outsourced dining models, the campus retains control of board pricing by guaranteeing a fixed-fee amount to the provider and accepting some level of risk for a sufficient number of board plan purchasers and retail food buyers. If the campus dining program also features local and national brand venues, the private vendor could oversee that relationship as well as operate more traditional dining venues.

Private dining operators are often willing to invest capital resources in the upkeep or construction of dining facilities, but generally with conditions. Most commonly, the more capital the private partner is asked to contribute, the longer the term of the negotiated contract to permit the operator a reasonable period of time to recoup the investment.

Numerous variations and conditions can include:

- hybrid models under which the campus chooses to self-operate some venues (e.g., the first-year dining hall) while outsourcing the rest;
- outsourcing all community dining venues to a single private operator, but directly contracting with other providers for individual retail venues;
- outsourcing with a fixed-fee amount, enabling the institution to retain decision making regarding costs, food quality, menu, and other programmatic elements of the dining program; and
- budgetary models that require the private operator to return a sum of money to the institution. In such models, food operators may have greater control over facilities, menu, dining hours, and meal plan charges.

A campus food services model offers insight into the tensions campus administrators navigate as they balance students' communal interests with consumer expectations. Lower board costs require lower food and operational costs, often at the detriment of the food program's perceived quality. Privatized dining models bring food services expertise to the campus, which may or may not translate into a more efficient operation. A preferred approach for any campus considers immediate cost implications; projected future capital needs; community dining quality and accessibility; nutritional concerns such as variability in diets; allergens; sanitary expectations; sustainability approaches; catering; and other commercial requirements.

Conference and Event Management

Another auxiliary service that may operate within student affairs or under the aegis of a business affairs unit is the conference and event management function. While many variations to this entity exist, most commonly the unit provides support to all campus events, including opening convocations, commencement, campus festivals and concerts, alumni events and reunions, career fairs, and a host of other campus conferences, meetings, and entertainment. The staff members in this unit arrange for furniture and tents, provide event registration services, coordinate parking and necessary transportation, and contract for all other needed services such as printing and publications, audio-visual and information technology, catering and meals, rental of campus and nearby spaces, and a host of other functions.

Several business models underlie a campus conference and event (C&E) operation. Under one variation, C&E operates as a fully self-supporting auxiliary. In such a model, the unit receives no funding from the institution and is expected to fully recover all expenses (and possibly contribute an amount to the institution) from charges to both campus and non-institutional customers. Thus, every service provided by C&E to academic departments, campus administrative operations, such as student affairs, athletics, and other campus clients, comes with a price. In many cases, student organizations are also charged for support of their events and activities with payment derived either from club and organization budgets, or advising or administrative units within student affairs. Sometimes, models favor higher pricing for services to non-academic or student events and even higher pricing for non-institutional activities.

Other variations exist that include assorted subsidies to underwrite student or academic events, rental charges from academic and other campus entities for use of space, and a host of internal recharges, including for campus police services and space access limitations.

C&E operations generally require effective partnership and collaboration with student affairs and other campus entities. Summer conference activities often include numerous sports camps hosted by the athletics and recreation department; precollege educational programs under the direction of academic units; and professional gatherings for which the campus simply provides accommodations, meals, and gathering spaces. Regardless of the model, student affairs will be a major player in C&E functions since campus residence halls, student dining facilities, student unions–centers, and other community meeting and gathering spaces are likely to be deployed in support of C&E activities. Many of these spaces and facilities are expected to serve summer students and hordes of C&E visitors, making effective and well-coordinated choreography of the use of dining, meeting, residence halls, and other venues essential. Additionally, financial models must consider wear and tear on campus facilities with appropriate pricing structures to ensure financial viability and continued investment in the campus environment.

The approach to C&E services depends on an institution's priorities and preferences. On some campuses, especially where C&E is under student affairs, a student-centric model will prevail; revenues from all non-student customers underwrite student events and support costs. Academic units may or may not be charged lower rates. On other campuses, students receive no favorable treatment and the burden for student-related events is borne by event budgets or through student affairs allocations.

Campus Card Services

It has been many years since a campus identification (ID) card was simply a piece of plastic with photo, campus affiliation, and expiration date. The plastic ID may no longer exist, replaced by the smart phone, wearable device, or other application that emulates the functionality of that plastic card. The transactional processes enabled by the card or other electronic devices have become far more complex and necessary on the contemporary college campus. The campus card or app may be deployed in any number of ways.

- **Identification.** The card or a smartphone depiction of the card is still an effective way to validate the identity of a student or other member of the campus community. The smartphone ID application adds multi-factor verification benefits through facial recognition and other biometric aspects of the phone's capabilities, which is one reason colleges and universities are moving toward options beyond the conventional ID card.

- **Building and parking lot access.** Card swiping and use of proximity access features to replace keys—through which a card's embedded signaling device unlocks a door or opens a gate—provide entry to residence halls, libraries, parking garages, classrooms, and other campus locations with restricted access. A substantial benefit of electronic access to buildings, storage facilities, music practice rooms, and a host of other spaces—beyond avoiding the complexity and expense associated with locksets, production, and distribution of keys and related record keeping—are the electronic records generated by each card, phone, or device transaction. These devices capture authorized accountability for each entry, frequency of access, predominant use schedules, and other relevant information. In addition, an electronic footprint enables users to be tracked for law enforcement or lifesaving purposes.
- **Dining access and purchases.** With both board and retail models, the campus ID serves as a cashless transactional technique, authorizing access to dining venues, registering meals, transmitting notices of retail purchases for subsequent billing, and debiting from prepaid accounts. Individual and aggregate information on various dining preferences are collected and, subject to legitimate and authorized uses, are analyzed for ongoing planning.

- **Bookstores and other retail purchases.** The campus ID and transactional device supports a cashless campus environment, enabling on-campus purchases and any purchases with off-campus partners authorized to use the system.
- **Library use.** Checking out a book? Click here. Want authorization to access the rare books collection? Click here. Need to make copies of this article? Click here.

The list of potential applications for the campus ID device is endless and basically applies to any transactional environment where the student or other member of the campus community needs recognition, authorization, and ability to conduct an applicable transaction. The device has morphed from an identification card to a credit–debit instrument, point-of-sale register, and campus umbilical cord.

Use of Data

What happens with the data collected and compiled by the campus card office? Armed with pertinent data, a campus dining operation can adjust operating hours to best meet market demands. With more granular data, such as detailed counts for specific food choices, offerings can be tailored to meet customer preferences. Of course, knowing french fries are in excessive demand does not mean a campus dining operation will always want to feed that desire. But, dining utilization data, coupled with other nutrition guidance, can lead to optimally balancing healthy communal models with consumer preferences.

Access to such data is not without controversy. Unbridled access to information should be of great concern to students, administrators, and others. The development and oversight of policies that preserve and protect the transactional records of students and other community members are critical. There will be circumstances when card utilization data is necessary to individual and community safety. Such situations include the need to find a missing student (card data can reveal if a student has been on campus and where that student has traveled or conducted transactions), the need to identify those who have engaged in inappropriate behavior in a venue where access is controlled by the ID device (data can reveal who has accessed the location), and the need to track event attendance to identify attendees. There are innumerable examples of circumstances where ID device data can be informative.

On many campuses, access to ID device data, other than for the unit for which the data are collected, will be limited to public safety officials to ensure proper handling of the information. Even units that are authorized to access individual and aggregate data should operate with policies and protocols that ensure proper storage of data, authorization of personnel permitted to see and use the data, and public dissemination of any information derived from the data.

Academic and Research Uses of Data

On many occasions, use of ID device data can serve faculty and graduate student research interests. Those who study food consumption patterns might find dining utilization data of great interest. Studies focused on sustainability might find campus transportation and parking data invaluable. A host of healthcare and well-being studies benefit from data derived from student use of health and counseling centers, albeit under strict privacy and confidentiality rules. Studies of student engagement benefit substantially from data revealing participation rates at activities and events. Campus IRB policies and procedures, coupled with institutional administrative protocols, should offer adequate protection of data and boundaries for data use for research purposes.

Cost Implications

There are significant cost implications depending on how student affairs, and all campus entities, partner with campus card services. As the housing operation moves from traditional locksets and keys to electronic access at main entrances and individual rooms, who pays for the equipment and who pays for the central systems that authorize and track access? As dining and other retail operations move to cashless transactions via the ID device, who pays for the expensive point-of-sale registers and other technologies that permit private credit and debit card use in addition to the campus ID device? The same questions are relevant for the campus libraries, parking and transportation, and every other device user.

Typically, the individual units cover the costs for unit transactional devices, and the campus card services operation charges a fee every time a transaction is made. Thus, for every door entry, food item swipe, parking gate opening, and library book borrowed, some charge is applied to the host organization, which may be recovered through fees administered by that group. Housing, dining, recreation center, and library fees are often used to cover both hardware and internal transactional costs.

As campus use of ID devices expands, all these issues—security of data, costs of installation and operations, and best practices for data utilization—become more critical and complex. Many of the emerging technological changes will also alter the landscape for campus ID devices and transactions. Imagine a future in which transactions completed by technology wearables or through implanted sensors, and empowered by AI applications, anticipate meal purchase preferences even before a student reviews a menu.

Athletics and Recreation

Rarely are intercollegiate athletics or campus recreation programs considered auxiliary. This section focuses on business models for these functions and the various points of connection with student affairs.

On some campuses, the full gamut of competitive sports, recreational activities, fitness programs, and other functions offered through athletics and recreation falls within student affairs. On other campuses, functions are split with intercollegiate athletics. Elite programs competing at the highest levels may report directly to the president or provost, and all recreational and fitness programs may be housed within student affairs. A third organizational structure, particularly at elite programs and institutions where courts, fields, and other facilities are shared by varsity athletes and the campus community, is one in which all functions report to a lead athletics and recreation staff member who reports to the president, provost, or other senior administrator outside of student affairs.

Funding Models

Funding models for these programs and facilities vary tremendously from campus to campus. The funding structure for the intercollegiate athletic program may be separate from recreation and fitness, but overlapping use of facilities may confound the independence of separate elements. Typically, the campus recreation and fitness program is supported through a combination of institutionally allocated central funds, either tuition or a portion of a state allocation to the institution, and a recreation fee. The percentage of funds derived from either source will vary based on the history, culture, and funding structures of the institution. In some states, students have the right to vote up or down any requests for fee increases and have significant influence on recreation budgets and proposed capital expenses.

Financial donations and fees collected from various services, such as summer sports camps, fitness classes, gymnasium rentals, playing fields, and other facilities, augment student fees and institutional contributions. Expenses include personnel costs and maintenance of facilities, equipment, and grounds. Recreation programs supported by these funds include intramural sports competitions.

Funding of intercollegiate athletics programs is generally far more complicated and differs substantially across the spectrum of institutional competitive environments. In the most complex circumstances, those schools that feature many varsity sports and compete at the highest levels obtain funding from many sources including:

- institutional allocations, particularly in support of athletic scholarships;
- donor support;
- commercial contributions in exchange for advertising at athletic competition venues and other locations, in campus publications and other communications, and sometimes even on players uniforms;

- a portion of athletic league revenues derived from tournament and national championship competition participation, including television and commercial business contributions;
- individual campus contracts with media, including television, radio, and online broadcasts and services; and
- auxiliary functions, including sports camps, clinics, and master classes.

Varsity sports generally fall into two groups: revenue sports and non-revenue sports. The fundamental difference is the degree to which revenue is generated versus requiring subsidies to cover expenses. Football and men's and women's basketball are recognized as the dominant revenue sports, often generating net revenues far in excess of their operating expenses. Most other sports teams, even with paid tickets and auxiliary revenues, still require a subsidy from the athletics department or the institution to balance their budgets. Across the country, very few intercollegiate athletics programs generate sufficient funds, despite revenues in the tens of millions, to fully cover the total costs of all varsity programs.

Funding of capital needs for athletics and recreation facilities is comparable to the model provided for residence hall funding. New or renovated facilities can be financed through public–private partnerships or through institutional or donor funds. With few exceptions, athletics programs often have access to commercial contributions not typically available for academic or student life facilities. Management of athletics and recreation programs requires unique expertise associated with athletic facilities, sports fields and courts, and compliance with extraordinarily complex compliance requirements.

Key Takeaways

The administrative and budgetary functions in the select operations highlighted in this chapter can be applied to many other areas at higher education institutions. Revenues can be derived from internal and external users, commercial and individual contributors, and institutional resources. Expenses include direct program or product delivery costs, contributions to various reserves, institutional taxes, and recovery costs for depreciation of various assets. Institutional policies and practices, often based in the culture and history of the institution, will dictate service and cost priorities, which may or may not advantage some community members.

Many auxiliaries also share unique and interdependent relationships with student affairs. Housing and dining services offer opportunities for student affairs to strengthen residential community development through communal dining environments and settings. The ambitions of student health and wellness centers to positively influence the well-being of students is inevitably enabled through partnerships with recreation and fitness. Both units benefit from dining programs that focus on nutrition and healthy dining. Student athletes are best served when all agencies that attend to their development as athletes and as students are well coordinated and aligned. Student events are optimally supported when club and organization advisors work collaboratively with technical expertise on event management, public safety, and related issues. Student affairs partnerships with academic affairs and auxiliary services units ensure best possible outcomes in the care and support of students and the entire college or university community.

CHAPTER 7

Legal Issues and Risk Management

The general counsel's office along with corporate risk management, internal audit, and compliance serve critical and essential roles with several common characteristics. Ultimately, they minimize institutional exposure and liability; protect college and university property, people, and other assets; and ensure institutional accountability and legal compliance.

This chapter begins with an understanding of the roles and responsibilities of each of these entities. Risk circumstances and legal consequences will then be explored, leading to a series of recommendations for student affairs practitioners.

General Counsel's Office

The general counsel's office is home to the institution's lawyers. Larger institutions, especially those with complex, academic medical centers, have sizeable offices with numerous attorneys. Smaller institutions might engage a local or national law firm to represent them as legal counsel. Fundamentally, the general counsel's role is to handle all legal claims on the institution, including formal litigation; to initiate proceedings when institutional legal rights are believed to have been violated; and to represent the institution and its employees in grievance and litigation proceedings associated with the performance of their duties. Legal counsel also advises on the development of relevant institutional policies, especially when liabilities are of consequence. Given the range of legal matters affecting colleges and universities, it is not uncommon for the general counsel's office to hire external experts with specialty legal practices as needed.

Corporate and Enterprise Risk Management

Risk mitigation is paramount in any organization and no less so in higher education. Institutional risk management staff are engaged in numerous activities to minimize the potential risks associated with the businesses of higher education. On many campuses, contracts for services or materials are reviewed by risk management staff, and possibly the general counsel's office, to identify language that puts the institution at risk for excessive charges, performance failures, and adverse service and delivery outcomes. Risk management staff also determine necessary and appropriate insurance requirements for contractors as well as conditions for insulating the institution from provider negligence and other failures. Risk managers determine appropriate processes and conditions for indemnification of the institution and its employees from adverse behaviors of external agencies and agents.

Internal Audit

While it is true that an aspect of internal auditors' roles is to review individual and departmental actions and expenditures to ensure propriety in processes and expenses, internal audit staff provide far more valuable services. The role of internal auditing is to assess the adequacy and effectiveness of processes for controlling financial and operational activities and managing associated risks. Internal audit experts review a host of practices to confirm alignment between policies and processes, to advise on optimal approaches to process execution as compared with institutional and normative benchmarks, and to uncover potential flaws and risks. The internal audit office is best seen as an agency that ensures preventative maintenance in addition to the more common presumption of forensic accounting subsequent to an allegation of financial misbehavior. For example, the charter for Duke University's Internal Audit Office specifies the office will determine whether the network of risk management, internal controls, compliance activities, and governance processes, as designed and represented by management, is adequate and functioning in a manner to ensure:

- Risks are appropriately identified and managed.
- Interaction with various governance groups occurs as needed.
- Significant financial, managerial, and operating information is accurate, reliable, and timely.
- Employee actions are in compliance with policies, standards, procedures, and applicable laws and regulations.
- Resources are acquired economically, used efficiently, and adequately protected.

- Programs, plans, and objectives are achieved.
- Quality and continuous improvement are fostered in Duke's control processes.
- Compliance risk is assessed, and the highest risks are included in the compliance work plan.
- Compliance risks are considered in institutional decision making.
- Significant legislative or regulatory issues impacting Duke are recognized and addressed properly. (Duke Office of Risk, Audit and Compliance, 2020, pp. 1–2)

Office of Compliance

The number and complexity of compliance requirements for colleges and universities can be overwhelming. Institutions are responsible for complying with an extraordinary array of rules and regulations across the campus. The following list includes 30 of the main topics for which detailed compliance requirements exist:

- Accounting
- Accreditation
- Athletics
- Campus safety
- Conflicts of interest
- Copyright and fair use
- Disabilities and accommodations
- Discrimination and affirmative action
- Donors and gifts
- Environmental health and safety
- Export controls

- Financial aid
- Foundations and affiliated enterprises
- Governance
- Grants management
- Higher Education Act
- Healthcare and insurance
- Human resources
- Immigration (international students and employees)
- Information technology
- Intellectual property
- International activities and programs
- Lobbying and political activities
- Privacy (student records)
- Program integrity rules
- Research
- Sexual misconduct
- Tax compliance
- Technology transfer
- Telecommunications

Many of these requirements are associated with the research enterprise of the university, but most of the topics have aspects that are applicable, if not central, to the work of student affairs. Those engaged in compliance review and reporting have critical roles to play in ensuring institutional conformity with all laws, rules, and regulations colleges and universities are obligated to satisfy. The university compliance office provides oversight of the program and the institutional processes that support compliance across the university. It investigates allegations of noncompliance to ensure the university compliance program meets the effectiveness requirements of the U.S. Federal Sentencing Guidelines and the U.S. Department of Justice Evaluation of Corporate Compliance Programs guidance. The compliance office or program assesses and monitors compliance and consistency with institutional risk tolerance and conducts centralized compliance reviews in areas of highest-priority compliance risks. Comparable to work by internal auditors, regular external reviews of compliance requirements by internal compliance staff and external experts mitigate the extreme risks and outcomes associated with compliance failures. Campus lawyers, unfortunately, spend a great deal of time dealing with legal consequences of compliance neglect and violations.

Despite best intentions and efforts, legal challenges are inevitable. The areas of campus conduct (especially sexual misconduct allegations), student housing, student physical and mental health, student group behaviors, and more have all experienced substantially expanded legal challenges, necessitating far more legal competency by student affairs practitioners. The best advice for vice presidents for student affairs: When in doubt, check with counsel.

A substantial amount of literature exists on law and higher education with a subset focused on the work of student affairs. This chapter covers a few examples with wide applicability and value.

Case Types and Jurisdictions

Judicial action can be either criminal or civil. Criminal cases are handled by local magistrates, judges, or possibly juries when the alleged violation is related to city, county, and state laws. For example, an allegation of a zoning violation regarding a campus property, when elevated to a legal challenge, would likely be handled by the municipal courts of the local city or county. Individuals charged with criminal violations would be subject to prosecution by the local district attorney's office through the local community's judicial system. More serious cases can be escalated for resolution to state-level courts. It is important to realize that each state, city, and county has laws and processes unique to the municipality, reinforcing the need for access to and reliance on the institution's general counsel's office.

Civil cases refer to allegations of violations of various forms of agreements. When families of students sue a college or university for what they believe to be a violation of the relationship between the student and the institution, the presumption is some written or implied agreement was breached, or the institution failed to fulfill its duty for which legal remedies are then sought. The legal relationship between a student and the institution—and the determination of whether there was a contract or not—varies from state to state. In addition, state cases brought by students often involve tort claims of emotional distress and negligence, which allows tort damages with the potential for significant monetary judgments.

Some cases involve allegations of violation of federal statutes, and these cases may be handled in federal courts under the jurisdiction of a federal judge. Such cases could involve violations related to Title IX and sexual misconduct, misuse of funds, and other serious breach allegations.

Records

There are substantial differences between public and private colleges and universities with regard to institutional records. Many states feature open records laws that essentially make any formal institutional record publicly accessible, including every email exchange and written correspondence. At private colleges and universities, such documents may not be available casually to the public. In a formal legal action, such as a lawsuit, many of these documents will be discoverable. Under subpoena from a judge, most email, written letters, reports, or notes on computers or in files will be revealed and potentially released to the attorneys of the plaintiff who initiated the lawsuit subject to some limitations where confidentiality must be preserved.

When a lawsuit is brought forward by an aggrieved party, the general counsel's office may issue a retention notice obligating staff not to delete or destroy any pertinent documents or materials. This point is worth repeating: Anything in writing and retained in physical or electronic records, whether in central files of the institution or locally on one's office or personal computer or hard-copy files, can be accessed when ordered by a court. This is all the more reason to be thoughtful in what information is recorded and retained.

Depositions

Should a lawsuit proceed to preparation for trial proceedings, parties to the matter may be summoned for a deposition, which is basically an interview of an individual who is presumed to have relevant information pertinent to the lawsuit. The interview is conducted under oath by the opposing attorney with all questions and responses recorded by an impartial court stenographer. Depositions are stressful and imposing. Everything said in a deposition may be admissible and consequential to a trial. A staff attorney from the general counsel's office or an attorney hired by the general counsel's office will be present at a deposition and will ensure appropriateness of legal processes, testimony, and the right to clarify unintended misstatements. Opposing attorneys may be confrontational and may require accountability for every record obtained through discovery.

Mediation, Settlement, and Trial

Appearance at a trial means that all other forms of informal resolution have been attempted without reaching a satisfactory resolution. In my 47-year student affairs career, I have never participated in a trial. Every case with which I was involved—and there were many—was either dismissed by a judge or resolved by a settlement. Generally, all parties to a lawsuit prefer to find resolution through some agreement to avoid a trial.

Some states require mediation prior to advancing a case to trial. An impartial mediator is hired and convenes both parties in nearby rooms. The mediator, who is often compensated by the institution, begins with a settlement proposed by the alleged aggrieved party and works to find a middle ground for agreement between the institution and the claimant. If successful, the agreement is brought to the attention of the court for closure.

With very expensive claims, the institution may consult with its insurance company, which would likely be obligated to pay the claim's cost should the claimant be successful in litigation. The insurer will weigh the risk and consequences of losing the suit against the proposed settlement costs. Often, the insurer will prefer to resolve the suit by accepting the financial settlement—presumed to be far less expensive than the potential costs of an expensive trial and more substantive judgment. For student affairs staff, a settlement can be a bitter pill to swallow when one firmly believes institutional behaviors were fully appropriate.

Relevant Laws and Competencies

There are several legal issues pertinent to student affairs and with which most staff should have some familiarity. The Family Educational Rights and Privacy Act governs the protection of students' educational records, which includes considerable information collected and stored by various student affairs units. The Health Insurance Portability and Accountability Act limits release of any medical records and applies to student health records maintained by a campus student health operation.

The U.S. Department of Education, under the Obama and Trump administrations, released multiple and conflicting advisory rules regarding sexual misconduct, which have had substantial implications for campus conduct processes and practices. The Office for Civil Rights, a unit of the U.S. Department of Education, oversees compliance with Title IX, which articulates the requirements for gender equity and response to allegations of sexual misconduct. Continued refinements and adjustments to campus roles and responsibilities should be expected, which necessitate ongoing review of institutional policies and practices.

Under the purview of the Office for Civil Rights, additional acts govern compliance with laws addressing disabilities and various forms of discrimination. The Jeanne Clery Disclosure of Campus Security Policy and Campus Crime Statistics Act, signed into law in 1990 (The Clery Act), requires any institution that accepts federal funds to track and report pertinent crimes on and near campus properties. The act obligates many campus officials, and notably student affairs practitioners, to be aware of safety behaviors and regulations for reporting and response.

The Drug-Free Schools and Communities Act, first passed in 1986, and also under the jurisdiction of the U.S. Department of Education, obligates colleges and universities to educate students and other members of the campus community about illicit use of drugs and alcohol. Annual public notification of this requirement, for example, is but one aspect of the act. As with most laws under the jurisdiction of the Department of Education, violations can affect access to federal funds.

The Higher Education Act (HEA), first signed into law in 1965, provides guidance and requires compliance in a variety of areas, including the proper disbursement of federal financial aid and accreditation guidelines. (The Clery Act is technically a subset of the HEA). The HEA is supposed to renew every 5 years but is often tied up in ongoing political controversies. Nonetheless, the provisions of the act, as was last approved, remain in force and continue to have significant impact on the higher education community.

The Americans with Disabilities Act (ADA) became law in 1990. The ADA prohibits discrimination on the basis of disabilities and ensures comparable rights and responsibilities for people with disabilities. Students with disabilities are protected by the ADA. Campuses are expected to, subject to some limitations, provide comparable access to all facilities and services. ADA compliance has far-reaching implications that affect every building, construction, or major renovation project. The extent to which an institution meets its ADA requirements sends a message about the value it places on full participation in the campus experience for all students.

Those involved in development and various forms of fundraising should be aware of laws associated with receipts of gifts from foreign entities. A host of laws applies to the management of personnel and guides hiring and termination discrimination, salary requirements, and unionization.

This sampling includes some of the most relevant laws applicable to colleges and universities that should be of concern and interest to student affairs. There are many more legal considerations at the state and local levels. Local municipalities have zoning laws that might affect renovation or construction projects. Individual states have requirements for drug and alcohol abuse prevention that augment federal requirements. Public institutions are subject to additional statewide requirements and obligations that affect campus conduct processes, open access to meetings, and confidentiality of communications.

Dynamic Nature of Laws and Legal Obligations

As complicated as these laws are as written, every action taken by a relevant oversight agency and new precedents established by subsequent litigation continue to mold and shape legislation. Despite the voluminous texts often associated with these acts and other legal guidelines and the plethora of guidance documentation issued to clarify meaning and processes, considerable gray areas often exist. Laws are constantly challenged and interpreted and then persistently reshaped by inevitable legislative and judicial tinkering. Institutional practitioners, guided by legal, risk, audit, and other areas of expertise, must stay current and competent on all that affects their campus roles and responsibilities. Many colleges and universities have government relations offices to monitor relevant local, state, and federal laws and proposed legislation and educate legislators and others on the implications of legislative and policy proposals.

What are the implications for the level of familiarity and expertise student affairs staff should have in this excessively complex legal environment? First, common sense should prevail. Anyone working in student affairs should at least be familiar with the existence of the acts and laws highlighted in this chapter. They should have a basic understanding of the nature of the acts and the general sphere of influence and obligations associated with these laws. As one's level of authority and responsibility expands, a more detailed awareness of relevant compliance requirements should be expected. Also, one should be aware of the implications of being personally named in a lawsuit or other legal action. Understand what support the college or university will provide and whether personal legal representation or coverage should be obtained. Consideration should also be given to carrying one's own liability insurance to augment support the institution provides.

Key Takeaways

The number of staff and offices working on risk management, compliance, and other legal matters is a consequence of the existing laws that impose a host of obligations on colleges and universities. Student affairs staff bear significant responsibilities for ensuring compliance with these laws and responding appropriately to various circumstances, including student behaviors that may be influenced by one or more of these laws. While the effort to remain in compliance with all legal obligations may seem excessive, failure to conform to the requirements under the statutes, acts, and laws is far more extreme. This simple mantra is offered as guidance to all practitioners: When in doubt, ask.

Reference

Duke Office of Risk, Audit and Compliance. (2020). *Office of audit, risk and compliance charter*. https://oarc.duke.edu/sites/default/files/documents/OARC%20Charter%20-%20APPROVED%2012.2.16.pdf

CHAPTER 8

Crisis Response and Management

This chapter focuses on the type and scope of crises that have historically affected college and universities. The array of crises requiring institutional attention seems to have expanded and escalated in recent years. Response to more common conventional crises is well worth considering as weather-related incidents, student political activism, and unexpected facility failures are inevitable. How does a campus and a student affairs division prepare for these circumstances?

Several incidents and situations in my career stand out as significant disruptors to my expected activities at the time. Fifty years from the day I began writing this chapter, May 4, 2020, my career in higher education was affirmed when students were horribly gunned down by the National Guard at Kent State University. As a result, campus protests over the actions of the United States in Vietnam launched a national strike in higher education, leading to the early closure of many colleges and universities. That spring, as in spring and fall 2020, graduating students were denied attending their formal commencement ceremony. My first tragic and unsettling crisis was when a student deliberately triggered a fire alarm in a residence hall. He waited until the corridor was full of exiting residents until he suddenly stepped into the hall and killed several students with firearms he hid in his room. He then took his own life.

Other campus crises that occurred during my career include:

- a strike by the union representing housekeepers and maintenance staff. I quickly learned how to clear trash chutes of stuck debris and move dumpsters to central collection areas.
- a major fire in the residence hall in which my wife and I resided. Immediate responses included finding alternate accommodations for residents as well as access to clothing, supplies, books, and other essential materials.
- supporting a student-hosted, national conference whose purpose was in direct opposition to my own values and beliefs. The fury from outsiders, who protested institutional unwillingness to prevent the gathering, was fierce and threatening.
- managing an alleged conduct violation involving use of racially charged language. This incident turned into a national cause celebre and essentially became my sole effort for a full academic year.
- involvement in a widely visible allegation of impropriety by an athletic team. This, too, consumed the time and energy of a full year and resulted in considerable legal action, notoriety, and recrimination.

- numerous circumstances involving loss of life though accidents, intentional acts of self-harm, and illnesses. On four occasions, I personally notified parents of the loss of a child.
- several large and dangerous gatherings of students protesting issues from apartheid in South Africa to climate action demands and a host of other political and global issues.

Other situations have included unexpected discovery of mold in residence halls requiring somewhat sudden and expensive renovations; small and large-scale infectious diseases; and various criminal behaviors both by and at students. I also have experienced numerous on- and off-campus celebrations, bonfires, pregame tailgates, and comparable events and activities at which excessive consumption of alcohol, use of other substances, and boorish behaviors from many students created rowdy, threatening, and unsafe conditions.

Most of my student affairs peers and I have experienced the terrible harms brought to members of the university community through expressions of bias and hate. Often, offensive behaviors by members of the campus community or unknown perpetrators from off campus trigger campus activism and protests. Responding to the harms legitimately felt by those targeted by the behavior requires sensitivity and thoughtfulness—especially when the politics of free expression are in play.

Inevitably, student affairs staff serve as the front line and first responders to many of these situations, ensuring effective crowd control, confiscation of assorted substances, and immediate care for those in jeopardy or harmed by the behaviors of others. Often, the aftermath of a crisis or tragedy requires ongoing and persistent support of the campus community and various cohorts of students.

While no two incidents are exactly alike, several lessons can be drawn from the events and crises I have observed, participated in, and led the response for.

- Preparation is essential. While many circumstances make preplanning impossible, most crises fall within a somewhat predictable array of situations. Students periodically or regularly gather in crowds either in objection to local or global matters, in celebration of an achievement, or simply for entertainment purposes.
- Planning is required for annual and predictable events, such as spring rituals and student group celebrations, as well as for sudden gatherings stimulated by some incident, political movement, or other flashpoint.
- With crowds of students, the presence and consumption of alcohol and other drugs should be presumed and planned for.
- Anticipation is key to managing both the expected and unexpected. Advance notice or familiarity with an event will not preclude unexpected circumstances. Sudden, unscheduled actions still require deployment of tactics for which preparation is key.
- Collaboration is critical. Within student affairs, planning should identify leadership roles and responsibilities, communications channels and expectations, and options for responses to various conditions and circumstances. Collaborative relationships with key institutional and municipal partners are also necessary. Stakeholders to many campus crises will include campus and local public safety, fire, and police departments; facilities operations; communications staff; medical and counseling personnel; and others.

- Campuses that regularly engage in emergency preparedness are best positioned to respond to student-related crises. Student affairs emergency preparedness should mirror campuswide efforts with a focus on conditions and circumstances most common to the student experience.
- Proper communications are required regardless of the magnitude or complexity of the event or crisis. Poor communications can turn a modest situation into a mammoth crisis, while effective communications can help contain the consequences of the situation. Planning is essential, and clarity on communications leadership, methods, and content is critical given the instantaneous, comprehensive, and distributed nature of social media. Internal communications, using student media, institutional publications, and other communications processes, are as important to manage as the external media. One of the occasions when I had to notify parents of the loss of their child was made far more urgent because students were immediately texting friends and others, forcing formal notification from the university before parents heard it from the social media grapevine.
- Positive relationships with student leaders can also contribute to effective management of an event or crisis. On many occasions, students have helped in such situations by conveying messages to activists, co-hosting town meetings and public forums on key matters, providing useful intelligence, and taking the lead with messaging and campuswide communications.

Staff Competencies and Expectations

Different conditions call for different expectations from student affairs staff. For some roles, job descriptions will include responsibility for response to various circumstances and situations. Student activities staff may be expected to be present at and support major student concerts, festivals, and events. Residence hall and housing staff often take the lead on large parties and other gatherings within residential facilities, and other staff members may be assigned responsibility for tailgating and athletic competition-related events.

Many circumstances necessitate support from student affairs staff and other members of the campus community. A controversial speaker whose presence is known to generate protests may require a team of faculty and staff to ensure both the presence and safety of the speaker and the proper rights of protestors. Similarly, student protests of institutional investment priorities at a board of trustees meeting may require the support of a team of faculty and staff to contain potential disruptions. The deputization of staff within student affairs and many other campus offices depends on formal policies for employees' services and roles, as well as on trust, informal relationships, and institutional conviction. Colleges and universities that lead with community-endorsed values and principles will find a large number of campus "volunteers" ready and willing to help manage controversial conditions and crises.

Not everyone has the capacity nor the willingness to walk into a crowd of students, and ask someone to cease from disrupting campus operations. No training overcomes the discomfort of those who simply cannot defuse a tense and potentially dangerous situation. Event and crisis management does not require everyone to be responsible for direct action and reaction; pre-incident identification of roles and responsibilities for key student affairs staff is important. Ongoing training is essential for anyone with formal responsibility or more limited functions to assist with crises. Table-top exercises and other simulations are useful ways to obtain and strengthen competencies necessary for crisis response and management.

Managing the Event or Crisis

In the heat of the moment, hours, days, or weeks of a situation or crisis, numerous questions and decisions must be considered. Responses to these questions and issues will vary by institutional characteristics, including private–public distinctions and legal obligations; resources available to cope with campus consequences; and preferences of campus leaders such as the governing board of the institution. The following examples offer guidance in dealing with a crisis.

Campus Protest or Activism

- If the protest is based on the presence of a controversial figure or group, do policies adequately articulate campus rules regarding time, space, and manner for guest appearances? Under what conditions, if any, would your campus prohibit a speaker, a performance, or some other campus presence?
- How will your campus react to a building occupation? Will campus leadership prefer to let students remain in place for an extended period of time or will students be involuntarily or forcibly removed?
- Are you prepared for the media onslaught likely to occur regardless of what actions you may take?

- Community reactions will vary depending on the specific circumstances of an incident and the forms of activism. Faculty, staff, and members of the local community may take a stance in support of or in opposition to the activists and, more likely, be divided by both perspectives. What position will your institution take regarding faculty and staff engagement with protestors and activists?
- Some situations draw supporters and detractors from outside the campus or the local community. What is your institutional position regarding access to the campus by nonmembers of the campus community? Can your campus be adequately secured if necessary?
- Under what conditions will your campus need to call for additional safety support from local or state public safety and police personnel? Are you prepared for the loss of control to non-institutional public safety, public health, or other outside players?
- Who will take point on discussions and negotiations with protestors?
- What student behaviors will rise to consideration for subsequent campus conduct violations or criminal accountability? Will all students who violate the campus protest policies be subject to prosecution?

Facility Failure, Fire, or Other Dangerous Conditions

- Are you adequately prepared for injuries or deaths associated with a structural failure or fire or some similar circumstance?

- Have you developed crisis response plans with local medical personnel and hospitals?
- Do you have options for relocation of staff offices, accommodations for student residents, preparation of food in dining facilities, or plans for laboratories, classrooms, or other kinds of facilities that could be affected by a major facility issue?
- How will communications be handled? Who notifies parents if students are affected by the crisis?

Health Issues

- Should your campus experience a breakout of an infectious disease, such as COVID-19, norovirus, mumps, meningitis, and other relatively common but serious illnesses, are you adequately prepared? Who takes point for your campus with a significant health crisis affecting students?
- Where can care be provided should the health crisis exceed the capacity of your campus health center and staff?
- Do you have facilities for quarantining students if necessary? Can food and other essential provisions and support be provided?

This small sample demonstrates the kinds of questions a campus, students, and student affairs divisions will face. Given various crisis conditions, decisions need to be made with little time to spare, and the potential number of crisis opportunities on campus exceeds the imagination. Preparing for technology breaches requires very different considerations than planning for the possibilities of weather-related treacherous conditions. One usually has lead time on the planned appearance of a provocative program or speaker versus the immediate campus outrage that might result from a racial incident, an act of violence, or a facility issue. Planning should anticipate as many incidents, issues, and crises as can be conceived for each campus environment, community, and conditions.

Key Takeaways

Advance preparation is critical to effective response when the inevitable crisis occurs. Some circumstances will be local to the campus or community while others may be connected to national or international situations. While it is impossible to anticipate every condition or crisis, colleges and universities should have the foresight to contemplate and create a plan, including various assigned roles and responsibilities, communications strategies, and emergency conditions. Student affairs staff, in particular, should regularly review crisis prevention and response plans for large gatherings of students, use and abuse of various substances, loss of a major facility, and processes associated with a variety of crisis circumstances. Practice may never lead to perfect, but practice may prevent disaster.

CHAPTER 9

Strategic Planning, Assessment, and a Culture of Evidence

Operating without strategic planning is akin to flying without a flight plan. In student affairs, strategic planning establishes both short- and mid-term objectives as well as a "blue sky" view to the more distant future. Effective strategic planning also provides pathways for achieving those objectives.

Student affairs strategic planning is distinctive in many respects. The work of student affairs encompasses widely diverse functions, some exclusively focused on the human development enterprise and others directed to assorted business and service industries. Stakeholders in student affairs work are equally diverse and include students, members of the campus community, parents and families, alumni, local citizens, and guests of the college or university. Finally, the operating practices for student affairs, including funding sources and uses, decision-making protocols, and accountability measures, feature complexities that differ from unit to unit and campus to campus.

Strategic planning in student affairs seeks to create harmony among these distinctions and ensure alignment between functions, people, and processes. Effective planning establishes priorities for fund allocation, capital investments, deployment of staff, and assignment of space. Strategic planning exposes divisional strengths and weaknesses, engages stakeholders in a collaborative venture, and contributes to staff enthusiasm for and confidence in the work ahead.

Student affairs roles and responsibilities exist within the institution's overall mission, vision, and goals, and its strategic planning processes should ensure alignment between the division's ambitions and vision with the broader institutional agenda. Thus, the ideal planning processes for student affairs comprise views above, below, and lateral to the organization.

The Planning Process

Numerous models for strategic planning are available across the landscape and literature of organizational development. For student affairs, several principles underlie planning buy-in and effectiveness.

- The timing and timelines for student affairs strategic planning are important. Effective planning takes time and should not be rushed; but a process that takes too long will suffer from planning fatigue and eventual disinterest from participants.

There will always be exceptions, but confining the formal planning period to an academic year seems reasonable. Ideally, the end point of a planning process should permit the outcomes to be immediately acted upon, suggesting careful timing alignment with budget cycles and other key operating decisions. It is critical to align the planning process with other major work demands to minimize the disruptive effect of adding strategic planning requirements to ongoing and essential work obligations.

- Productive planning engages many if not most members of a student affairs organization, but not everyone can fully participate and even fewer people can be assigned leadership roles. Senior student affairs leaders must be sensitive to finding the right balance between those who have explicit roles in the planning processes versus those who indirectly participate. Ultimately, the goal is for collective buy-in from all staff members regardless of their level of participation in the process.
- Communication is key to achieving desired buy-in from student affairs staff as well as other institutional stakeholders and partners. Effective communication is bidirectional, enabling everyone affected by the planning efforts to contribute viewpoints and reactions and persistently keeping them informed of progress and outcomes throughout the process. Communications need to be frequent, informative, and inspirational as the process unfolds and evolves.
- Candor and honesty are critical ingredients to any strategic planning process, but even more so for human services

organizations such as student affairs. A common starting point for the planning process might be departmental self-assessments: Each unit conducts an internal review of strengths, weakness, opportunities, and threats (SWOT). Strengths could include elements such as access to sufficient resources, the presence of adequate and competent personnel, and viable space and locations within the institution. Weaknesses might incorporate the opposite of strength elements but could also suggest poor alignment or cooperation with necessary partner units, leadership challenges, or reputational limitations that adversely affect student supports. Consideration of opportunities enables units to think about emerging ideas and needs and contemplate possible new interventions and treatments. The discovery of threats enables repositioning of all departmental assets and approaches to minimize potential negative consequences and influences ahead. The development of a genuine SWOT analysis requires thoughtful and truthful self-reflection.

Forms of strategic planning abound as does the number of consultants and consulting practices available to support the effort. Larger institutions often provide planning facilitation through its human resources organization. Some student affairs organizations, especially those that have embraced strategic planning as an ongoing function, have added planning specialists to their staffing models. Absent a role with explicit planning responsibility, a lead person might be identified who, with the support of a cross-division steering committee, could direct the divisional strategic planning process. The leadership of the student affairs division, especially the vice president for student affairs (VPSA), must take overall ownership for the work, convey confidence in the effort, and commit to advancing outcomes for the process to succeed.

With considerable variation, student affairs strategic planning might begin with communication to the division that introduces the planning intentions, rationale, and processes. Some form of community gathering, such as a town meeting of sorts for student affairs staff, provides opportunities for further information-sharing as well as responses to questions. A next step might include the commissioning of a self-assessment SWOT analysis. One particular challenge for a student affairs self-study is how to benchmark achievements or productivity.

Benchmarks

Benchmarks can be thought of as performance standards against which any effort can be compared. It makes perfect sense when measuring the productivity output of a widget machine: The average production across a thousand widget machines is X. A single machine that produces less than X is underperforming, and the machine that exceeds X goes beyond expectations. Applying productivity measures to the work of counselors, mentors, advisors, teachers, residence hall housekeepers, and food services providers is far more complicated. Complicated does not mean impossible, and a contemporary student affairs division should deploy comparisons with industry benchmarks in its self-assessment processes.

Many tools and programs exist to aid in benchmarking student affairs—though not nearly as many as are truly needed. One of the most highly regarded and frequently referenced set of benchmarks are those offered by the Council for the Advancement of Standards in Higher Education (https://www.cas.edu/standards). Many others have been designed specific to various programs and practices in student affairs, often by distinctive professional associations. Other comparison options exist through institutional consortium partnerships, statewide data reporting processes, and federal data collection efforts. In my experience, student affairs reviews and self-assessments have lacked adequate benchmarking analyses, which is often due to specious arguments about the quality and use of those benchmarks. It is high time student affairs divisions take benchmarking of outcomes and productivity seriously.

Self-Studies

With sufficient resources and adequate time, departmental self-studies can be complemented by external reviews conducted by subject matter experts from peer institutions, professional associations, or other stakeholder entities. The additional information that could be gleaned from external reviews would be of considerable value, but the process will likely take far more time.

Even as self-assessments are underway, the steering committee should review and reflect on broader influences on the work of the division. Consideration should be given to institutional plans and aspects of those plans that set operating foundations and expectations for the student affairs division. Institutional priorities govern future access to funds and capital investments, teaching and research directions, enrollment expectations, and other intentions and aspirations. These intentions influence every aspect of an institutional and student affairs planning process and draw out implications that affect the division's work ahead. These implications, converted to influential principles and practices, should guide subsequent departmental and divisional strategic planning.

The strategic planning process attempts to integrate internal needs analyses, SWOT reviews, external examinations, and institutional plans in the development of forward-looking plans for student affairs departments and the division. Tough questions are asked at this point: What units must grow and what can shrink or consolidate? With limited access to capital resources, what spaces and facilities deserve attention over the next few years? How does one best take advantage of collective and unit-specific strengths and opportunities while minimizing or avoiding weaknesses and threats? Who are the people to entrust with the future of the enterprise, and who needs to be nurtured out?

Executing the Plan

The development of a student affairs strategic plan is an awesome achievement. Unless the plan finds a final resting place on a shelf in someone's office or in a server file high in a distant cloud, processes for executing plan provisions and tracking achievement and effectiveness come next. There is not a single approach to effective plan implementation, but common elements include identification of a point person to lead and track the effort, establishment of regular reviews of progress, and development of ongoing assessment processes for measuring achievement and outcomes.

Point Person

The staff member with a dedicated planning role or staff member assigned to that role obviously own the responsibility for helping translate the planning language to unit-specific interventions. The strategic plan might speak to support for underrepresented students, but how a counseling center advances that objective will differ from a career center's approach. Converting a divisional strategic plan to explicit programs and processes within each student affairs unit is critical to planning success. The leadership of each unit, working with the staff member assigned overall responsibility to implement the plan, should develop local and measurable objectives to advance the work of that organization consistent with the plan. The divisional strategic plan should lead to departmental plans that reflect the specific and explicit directions for each unit.

Creating a Successful Strategic Plan

The following guidelines contribute to a successful and effective strategic plan.

- Develop and stick to a timeline.
- Engage, but control, stakeholder participation in the process.
- Presume every idea to be more expensive and complex than the plan proposes.
- Preview plans (VPSA role) with institution leaders and peers.
- Prepare to pivot as the unexpected inevitably transpires.
- Celebrate the development of the plan, and acknowledge the effort and contributors.

Regular Reviews

An effective strategic plan is a living document that offers a clear roadmap for the work of the organization. Just as maps feature multiple routes and various endpoints, the strategic plan must offer sufficient flexibility and adaptiveness to accommodate assorted influences that necessitate plan adjustments. Clearly, unexpected crises disrupt strategic planning, forcing just-in-time changes to meet complex and unexpected needs. However, even absent catastrophic conditions, unplanned circumstances that require pivots and punts should be anticipated.

Preparing for the unexpected does not mean anticipating every kind of crisis or situation, but practicing for potential or likely scenarios is recommended. In the realm of strategic planning, being prepared means establishing systems and processes that enable effective response to sudden or timely conditions. Identifying who will be "on point" is a starting place, but establishing a team to regularly review plan progress and make adjustments is also important. Ongoing review of a student affairs strategic plan offers more than the capacity to address challenges and crises. It assures continued exposure to the plan, visibility for the plan, persistent attention to plan progress, and the opportunity to develop communications strategies for sharing plan efforts and achievements with student affairs' stakeholders.

Assessment

Benchmarks are a key aspect of departmental self-analyses. Benchmarks have utility only if departments have established metrics to measure progress. Achievement metrics will differ dramatically among student affairs units, but are essential to gauging progress and success. A few aspects of assessment are worth noting.

- **Measuring inputs does not substitute for measuring outputs.** Counting the number of students who may attend a particular program will not stand as proxy for measuring the knowledge obtained at that program. Knowledge of the alcohol consumption patterns of an incoming class of students helps with developing risk reduction interventions, but it will not predict the impact of those efforts.
- **Measures of behavioral intentions offer limited value given the low correlation with actual behavior.** If you want to know if training actually impacted students' behavior, you cannot only ask them what they are likely to do under various conditions. You have to determine their actions when exposed to that condition to know if the training was effective.
- **A single assessment effort will tell you something about a cohort of students (or others) based on their unique experiences and conditions.** If you want to know the ongoing effectiveness of any treatment, measurements must be ongoing and persistent. Multiyear trend analyses have more value as evidence of progress than a one-time assessment effort.
- **Measuring progress on complex student development efforts cannot be casual or simplistic.** Measuring progress on advancing racial awareness, diminishing sexual misconduct, or elevating the population mental health of a student community requires explicit expertise, intensive commitment to the effort, and a willingness to accept and react appropriately to the findings.

A Culture of Evidence

Organizations that exhibit a culture of evidence reflect an innate and habitual intentionality about evaluation and assessment. In such organizations, behavioral norms include the development of assessment plans to accompany new program proposals, regular and public discussions about assessment strategies and implications, and effective use of a wide variety of assessment data, including those derived from broader institutional and external sources. A culture of evidence in a student affairs division suggests staff frequently ask: How do we know if we are accomplishing our objectives? Are we exploring alternative answers for that question?

High-quality strategic planning coupled with a strong culture of evidence are key attributes of excellence in any organization, particularly human services organizations like student affairs. Establishing an evidence-based approach to student affairs work has proven to be challenging not entirely because of resistance to assessment but because measurement and assessment of student affairs work take considerable time and effort and can be burdensome to people and agencies struggling to meet student and community needs. Staff members are confronted with the need to postpone or eliminate some responsibilities to make time and space for evaluation efforts. There are no easy solutions, but there are options.

All colleges and universities engage in ongoing comprehensive assessment. Much of it is mandated by federal and state agencies for various reporting obligations while other aspects are locally determined. Most campuses have some form of an institutional research office that coordinates institutionwide assessment efforts and takes the lead on various consortium evaluation processes. Surveys of alumni, students, and other constituents are usually included in such assessment efforts. I have always marveled at the depth and breadth of information readily available on each campus and have simultaneously been dismayed by how rarely those data are accessed and used. There is a treasure trove of information regularly collected, compiled, and analyzed that can and should be accessed by student affairs.

Developing a culture of evidence in student affairs means promoting measurement and assessment not as secondary or supplemental to all other efforts. In such organizations, measurement and assessment are recognized as essential, sought after as evidence of progress, and relied on for programmatic guidance and excellence. Flying without a flight plan leads to endless circling or worse. A student affairs division with a deep commitment to evidence-based planning and implementation asks critical questions, gathers relevant information, and operates from a perspective of accountability.

Key Takeaways

Authentic strategic planning is efficient, collaborative, and purposeful. All too often, student affairs strategic planning fails because the process was overly cumbersome, ill-defined, and far too granular to be strategic. Planning processes collapse under the weight of well-intended participatory requirements that favor inclusion of every voice without effective means to incorporate all those perspectives in the plan.

An effective planning process is inclusive, collaborative, and nimble, deploying a variety of quantitative and qualitative data collection. An effective planning process reveals timelines, boundaries that may be non-negotiable and reasons why, and alignment with institutional plans. An effective planning process has well-defined leadership, structure, and participants, and it includes measures by which the plan will be evaluated. Developing a divisional culture of assessment further ensures continued reflection on the plan and its intended and unintended outcomes.

CHAPTER 10

Communications

Student affairs professionals must deal effectively with many types of communications, including regular and ongoing messaging and all-too-frequent unplanned and crisis communications to both internal and external stakeholders. The messaging processes may differ for students, parents, alumni, and the many other constituents served by student affairs. With ubiquitous social media and a 24/7 news cycle, the communications game has changed substantially in recent years. These issues and needs are explored further in this chapter.

Internal Communications

Throughout my career, whenever staff were queried about strengths and weaknesses in the student affairs organization, internal communications always emerged as one of the weakest functions. Employees at all levels, but mostly those in entry-level or next-level roles, would note they felt uninformed and unclear about the organization's direction and objectives. This perspective, one I recall from my earliest days as a student affairs professional, may be endemic to staff who are at a distance from student affairs leaders—especially at institutions with large and soloed staff. Every year, those of us in leadership roles at my institution would commit to better attention to internal communications, staff engagement at all levels, and enhancements in participatory governance. Subsequent employee workplace assessments would reveal staff frustration with divisional lack of transparency topping the list of weaknesses—again.

Communications in student affairs is as much art as science. Given the diverse array of student affairs stakeholders, information sharing must be carefully considered and implemented in ways that appropriately inform, convey sentiments as needed, offer viewpoints relevant to different campus constituencies, invite desired but bounded feedback, and reflect required and preferred confidentiality. As a vice president for student affairs, I felt a particular obligation to ensure institutionwide familiarity with and support for the work of the division. I also believed it was my responsibility to be as informed as possible about every aspect of the university that could have some relation to student affairs work.

Fulfilling that role of lead communicator and cheerleader takes considerable effort. It means curating reports, newsletters, and opportunities to identify those of interest and value to others. Information regularly distributed to deans, department heads, committee chairs, senior officers, and other campus constituents will ensure their familiarity with student affairs work and stimulate their interest in and support for student affairs efforts. Being deliberate about advancing the work of a student affairs division also requires broad awareness and review of information across campus to select and be aware of relevant work outside the division. In time, these expectations of communicating up and absorbing pertinent external communications can be conveyed to the leadership team and become a core component of the overall divisional communications strategy. It is undeniable there is a political angle to any communications strategy, which is critical to organizational success.

A Need to Know

An ongoing communications struggle for any organization is determining who needs to know what and when. In a student affairs organization, information persistently flows in and out of the division in every direction and across and within every unit. Those divisions fortunate enough to have the resources to employ a communications leader or team have some capacity to manage this flow of information and be somewhat deliberate about communicating essential and appropriate information to key stakeholders. Many student affairs organizations rely on distributed or serendipitous models of information sharing, which limit the deliberateness of regular and timely communications. Several principles can help coordinate divisional communications strategies and practices.

- A communications strategy should be part of an overall strategic planning effort. A divisional strategic plan (as described in Chapter 9) provides the roadmap for departmental and divisional operations and activities and should also serve as the roadmap for the communications plan. Embedded in the strategic plan should be expectations for data collection and internal and external information dissemination about progress and roadblocks related to organizational intentions. Progress reports and strategic plan updates can take the form of internal newsletters, memos or blogs, divisional town meetings, presentations to project team leaders, and other information-sharing approaches. Regular and reliable updating of strategic plan progress and outcomes inspires persistent attention by student affairs staff, external partners, and leaders to the divisional plan.

- On any given day on most campuses, something modestly or significantly disruptive to the day's plans will happen. In Chapter 8, the nature of crisis management was addressed, and certainly every crisis yields an opportunity, if not an obligation, to keep people informed. Issues of concern transpire daily at levels far below crisis conditions and will be of general interest. These may include staffing or organizational changes, unique and interesting programs, notable achievements by students or other community members, or equally notable problematic behaviors by students or others. The institution's communications office will feature various aspects of campus news of note, which can be routed to student affairs colleagues. Someone in the student affairs division should be assigned responsibility for curating campus and divisional news and establishing internal communications practices for proper dissemination of that information.
- Communications convey messages, both intended and unintended. The absence of a response to a racial incident can convey a far more powerful and potentially deleterious

message than a statement condemning the incident. The delicate matter of announcing a student death without revealing the cause of death (usually suicide) haunted me on far too many occasions. A national or international disturbance or crises requiring a statement from the VPSA when other more senior staff decline to comment can prove to be equally delicate and never quite right. The inclusion of one party to an offense or victimization could open up accusations of neglect of comparable painful impact on others. With the support of and guidance from institutional communications experts, student affairs communications staff, and others with relevant expertise and information, reasonably effective communications approaches can be developed.

- Time is an enemy to proper communications, especially subsequent to an incident or unexpected situation. With ubiquitous photo and video capture, hyper-fast transmission of information, and a vast array of news outlets, the opportunity for an institution focused on the care of students to pause and reflect before issuing a statement or sharing information has long passed. Speed is of utmost concern, but beware of launching an error-filled narrative of a circumstance. Even if the campus shares information in a timely manner, one can expect to read or see alternate versions.

Impact of Social Media

Social media has fundamentally and permanently altered the landscape of communications in all domains. An army of young people equipped with a plethora of online broadcast tools can spread messages faster and further than any institutional communications process. There are many societal benefits to instant and viral transparency of circumstances and subsequent discourse about implications of various situations, but the deleterious effects of gossip sites, inadvertent and deliberate sharing of misinformation, and shaming or unsubstantiated criticism of individuals has yielded harmful and tragic outcomes as well. Student affairs must certainly have a presence on various social media sites, but caution and careful consideration of conditions and opportunities should be exercised. A divisional strategy for social media should identify those with authority to post messages and those who understand proper use and boundaries for social media communications. There is a distinction between sharing notice of activities and events online versus offering commentary, criticism, and opinions about matters. Many can be empowered to communicate the former, but very few should be permitted to represent the student affairs organization and the university with communications that express an institutional position. This stance is not limited to social media communications, but it is certainly amplified due to the ubiquitous nature of these applications.

Clarity of distinction between personal and institutional social media presence is essential, and consequences for personal postings that may be deemed improper should be clarified as well. As with so many situations, transparency of expectations in advance of an incident is always preferred.

Confidentiality

Not all information can be shared. On those occasions when confidentiality is required, student affairs leaders must be prepared to respect legal and ethical boundaries. Confidentiality may be required about students' health conditions, planning and other policy decisions not ready for public dissemination, and personnel matters. Media training for the staff member selected to convey information is critical along with skills development in filtering messages and information that should not be shared.

Communicating with Journalists

Communications with the media, including campus news outlets and local, national, and international media affiliates, merit discussion. I always gave student news outlets far more access to information than external media. I very much respect the importance of student newspapers and other campus media as a laboratory for teaching. For novice campus reporters and commentators, misquotes, misconceptions, and missed opportunities are fairly common—as they are for all media. Several practices with student media help ensure more accurate reporting.

- When contacted by a student reporter about some circumstance for which there is history and previous news stories, ask if they have reviewed all previous accounts and reports. Inevitably, student reporters may not have taken the time to fully apprise themselves of all the backstories related to a topic. Request they familiarize themselves with all previously reported information before engaging with student affairs. This request might be perceived as off-putting, but student reporters typically are appreciative of the advice.

- Avoid off-the-cuff interviews. Sometimes, it is advisable to ask for interview questions submitted in writing. The questions tend to be more thoughtful, and a written response to the reporter ensures accuracy in quotes and details.
- A face-to-face interview is better than phone conversations. Message nuances are best expressed with eye contact. Establish clear boundaries and expectations for the interview upfront: length of time, focal areas, and aspects of the topic for which you cannot comment.
- Pick your battles carefully. Student media and other platforms relish investigative journalism, and good news stories are sometimes hard to find. Blatant errors should be brought to the attention of the reporter and, if necessary, escalated to editors or advisors. Be judicious with your criticism. It is best not to debate every misquote or misinterpretation of circumstances.

Communications with noncampus outlets should be cleared by and managed through campus news and communications experts. Each appearance I made in front of a television camera was authorized by university news and communications representatives, who coordinated ground rules and conditions as appropriate. Above all, never say anything to a reporter you are not prepared to see in print.

Key Takeaways

The art and science of student affairs communications is very much a moving target. Overall, communications outlets of all forms are expanding. Despite best efforts to thoughtfully and deliberately manage dissemination of information; issuance of statements and reports; and responses to incidents, situations, and crises, a fair amount of student affairs communications will be reactive, defensive, and perceived as insufficient, insensitive, and uninformative. A communications strategy for any student affairs unit that is as candid and transparent as possible; is accessible, visible, and informative to its many constituencies; and is as focused on internal communications as external stakeholders is a worthy accomplishment.

CHAPTER 11

Student Affairs: An Uncertain Future

I am neither an optimist nor a pessimist. I like to think of myself as a realist. As a realist, I expect occasions of progress periodically interrupted by assorted challenges and crises. I plan for forward movement but anticipate episodes of regression. In my 47 years of student affairs work on several university campuses, I experienced periods of stability regularly disrupted by segments of instability. A career grounded in realism means hoping for tailwinds but not being surprised by headwinds. The goal is to experience far more steps forward than back.

Higher education is at one of those frequent crossroads where its future is subject to internal and external conditions that are difficult to discern and challenging to prepare for. The COVID-19 pandemic dramatically altered the educational landscape, and expanded use of synchronous and asynchronous online education is likely a permanent feature of higher education. A new generation of presidents, provosts, deans, and other college and university leaders recognizes the need for educational reforms that better align didactic and experiential learning; ensures graduates access to work and career pathways; addresses societal challenges, including racial, ethnic, socioeconomic, and other social divides; considers the perils of climate change, poverty, hunger, and homelessness; and secures the health and well-being of students, faculty, and staff. This new generation of leaders recognizes the cost of education cannot continue to rise unchecked as public funds allocated to teaching and research continue to decline.

The implications for student affairs and its related roles and responsibilities are substantial. The optimist in me sees continued expansion for student mental health support, equity and justice, and a host of social skills development. When I wear my rose-colored glasses, I see further investment in staff and services to ensure student success, improvement and expansion of student-focused campus facilities, and a continued presence and voice of student affairs staff and leadership in all critical decision-making discussions.

The pessimist in me worries about stringent budget cuts and the likelihood of a disproportionate allocation of those cuts to student affairs; the shrinkage of the number of high school graduates anticipated in the years ahead combined with significant declines in international student enrollments, contributing to administrative retrenchment; and distrust in the competencies and capacities of student affairs leaders to effectively manage major administrative operations. The pessimist view suggests dramatic curtailment of some student affairs functions.

My more realistic view leads me to believe that, while change is inevitable, the forms of change will be unique to each institution and to leadership preferences. I also fervently believe these preferences and the subsequent organizational consequences can be influenced by the student affairs community, including those in leadership roles, professional associations, and graduate preparation programs educating the next generation of practitioners and influencers.

For student affairs practitioners-educators to be influential in the future direction of individual campuses and higher education at large, several things must happen.

- Student affairs needs an identity fix. The profession cannot be perceived as isolationist in claims of unique expertise in student growth and development. The profession cannot assert ownership of experiential education. The profession cannot assert exclusive advocacy for the needs of disadvantaged, underrepresented or marginalized students. To be sure, student affairs work must continue in all these domains, but student affairs staff must expand partnerships with academic, auxiliary, and other campus entities to be appreciated as individuals and units with distinctive expertise whose work is amplified when collaborating with institutional partners.
- Student affairs practitioners–educators need to be more competent administrators and managers. Those who aspire to leadership roles need far more skills development than those who avoid managerial roles. Every staff member should have a basic understanding of the financial flows and challenges

of the institution and the student affairs division. Risk management is a universal obligation for which basic awareness and competency are essential. An understanding of effective supervision and how best to react to poor supervision is equally important. Professional development to compensate for inadequate skills development is critical.

- Student affairs leadership must do whatever it takes to obtain and retain seats at the adult tables. The vice president for student affairs must be recognized as a broad, serious, and comprehensive higher education thinker who is more than competent to represent human, fiscal, and structural resources with the capacity to represent student affairs' voices up as well as institutional decisions down.
- The professional associations representing student affairs must make adjustments to broaden their advocacy for skills development and competencies and diminish their contributions to the isolationism. Consideration should be given to consolidation of various associations or, at least, to far better connectivity among the plethora of student affairs subgroups and to umbrella associations such as NASPA–Student Affairs Administrators in Higher Education. Advancing student affairs as a profession of competent managers and educators must be high priority in the months and years ahead if an optimistic viewpoint is to be realized.

I want to take a moment to address those readers who may serve as faculty in higher education, student affairs, and related graduate preparation programs. With high regard for the extraordinary efforts to prepare the next generation of practitioners and educators in student affairs, I share my concern about how underprepared I have found new professionals to be with regard to the topics covered in this book. This noble profession has deep roots in the counseling field, and more recent attention and focus has been paid to education and training in human (student) development, especially with regard to diversity and inclusion. But diminishing attention to the core business functions of student affairs within the curricula of graduate training programs imperils the profession and student affairs professionals.

The power of the student affairs profession lies in its ability to understand the needs of those whom the profession serves, to advocate to decision makers at all levels on behalf of students, and to have the credibility and authority to execute all actions necessary to accomplish planned objectives. The skill sets referenced in this book are intended to serve the latter need—to equip student affairs practitioners–educators with the means to analyze circumstances, alter environments, invest in structures and programs, and lead campus progress.

The Author

Larry Moneta served as vice president for student affairs at Duke University from 2001 to 2019 when he retired to a life of consulting, teaching, and grandparenting. At Duke he led the central planning, policy formation, and coordinating agency for the university concerning student issues. Moneta worked in student affairs on a variety of campuses before joining the Duke community in August 2001, most recently at the University of Pennsylvania as associate vice president for campus services from 1997 to 2001 and associate vice provost for university life from 1992 to1997.

In addition to his administrative duties, Moneta teaches a wide variety of courses, consults for institutions across the country, and presents regularly at conferences and workshops. He has been an active member of NASPA–Student Affairs Administrators in Higher Education, ACPA–College Student Educators International, and other organizations, serving NASPA most recently as a member of its National Academy for Leadership and Executive Effectiveness

Board and as a member of the NASPA Foundation Board. He received his EdD and BS from the University of Massachusetts, and his MEd from Springfield College.

Moneta's publications include *The Influence of Technology on the Management of Student Services* (Jossey-Bass, 1998), *Future Issues in Serving Students at Metropolitan Universities* (Jossey-Bass, 1998), *Future Trends in Student Affairs* (NASPA, 2003), and the coauthored chapter "When Expectations and Realities Collide: Environmental Influences on Student Expectations and Student Experiences" in *Promoting Reasonable Expectations: Aligning Student and Institutional Views of the College Experience* (Jossey-Bass, 2005).

In 2020, Moneta became the board chair of ShalomLearning, a nonprofit providing curricula, teacher training, and an online platform for supplementary Jewish education. He also became a member of the Jewish Grandparents Network Advisory Board and the advisory board of Jewish Changemakers, a leadership development fellowship for Jewish college students and recent graduates presented by the Jewish Federations of North America.

Index

A

Achievement metrics, 129–130
ACPA–College Student Educators International, 70–71
Alcohol use, 107, 108, 114
Alumni, 4–5, 25
Americans with Disabilities Act (ADA, 1990), 107–108
Apps as ID cards, 88
Architectural firms, 58–61, 62
Artificial intelligence (AI), 79–80
Assessments, 75–76. *See also* Strategic planning and assessment
Athletics
 auxiliary services and, 93
 building projects and, 56, 64, 95
 funding models and, 93–95
Audits, 15, 99–100
Auxiliary and other operations, x, 81–96
 athletics and recreation, 93
 campus card services, 88–90
 conference and event management, 86–88
 cost implications, 92–93
 data usage, 90–92
 food services, 83–86
 funding models for, 93–95
 origins and models, 81–82
Award ceremonies, 35

B

Bargaining agreements, 7, 84
Benchmarks, 125–126, 129–130
Benefit plans, 7, 35
Best practices
 for financing and budgeting, 14–15
 for hiring, 44–45
Bias
 explicit, 43
 fit of employees, determining, 44
 hiring practices and, 43
 implicit, 33, 43
 salary equality and, 35
 talent identification and, 43
Bookstores, 90
Budgeting. *See* Financing and budgeting

Buildings and grounds. *See* Facilities management

C

Campus administrative practices and preferences, 25–27
Campus card services, 88–93
Campus governance models, 24–25
Campus housing
  construction of. *See* Construction projects
  design of, 52–53, 58–61
  design options for student affairs and, 26
  long-range planning for, 9
  renovation of, 57
  revenue generation from, 51
Campus master planning, 50–52, 66
Campus media, 141–142
Campus protests or activism, 113, 117–118
Capital projects, 8–10. *See also* Construction projects
Career centers, 75, 82
Cash
  best practices for, 14
  expenditures, 13–14
  expense violations, 13
  fee payments and, 14
  reserves of, 15, 55–56
Civil court cases, 103
Clery Act (1990), 106–107
Cloud storage, 74
Collaboration, 114
Commercial partners, 10, 11, 56
Communications, x, 135–143
  confidentiality of, 140–141
  emergency preparedness and, 115
  internal, 135–137
  with media and journalists, 141–142
  need to know status and, 137–139
  social media impact and, 139–140
  strategic planning and, 123
  subpoenas of, 104
Competencies
  in crisis response and management, 116–117, 147–148
  in legal issues and risk management, 106–108
  professional associations and, 148
  in technology, 70–71
Compliance office, 100–102
Conference and event (C&E) management, 5, 82, 86–88
Confidentiality. *See* Privacy and confidentiality
Construction projects
  budget development for, 8–10
  building design and, 52–53, 58–61
  case for starting, 54–55
  financial models for, 55–58
  managing, 61–67
  zoning laws and, 108
Continuous learning, 40–41
Contractors, 62, 98
Corporate and enterprise risk management, 98
Council for the Advancement of Standards in Higher Education, 126
Counseling services, 27
COVID-19 pandemic, xii, 72, 145–146
Crime, 106–107
Criminal court cases, 102–103
Crisis response and management, x, 111–120
  campus protests or activism, 117–118
  examples, 112–113
  facility failure, fire, or dangerous conditions, 118–119
  fiduciary risk assessment and mitigation, 11–14
  health issues, 119–120
  lessons for, 114–115
  staff competencies and expectations, 116–117

Culture of evidence, 131–132
Culture of organizations, 18, 28–29

D

Data management. *See also* Privacy and confidentiality
   academic and research uses of data and, 75–76, 91–92
   for auxiliary and other operations, 90–92
   backup, 73
   cloud storage, 74
   records laws and, 103–104, 106
   strategic planning and, 138
   student privacy and, 74–76, 106
   third-party partnerships for, 76–78
Debt-financed construction, 10, 56
Demographic changes, 19–21
Department of Education, 106–107
Department of Justice Evaluation of Corporate Compliance Programs, 102
Depositions, 104–105
Design of campus housing
   achieving success in, 59–61
   architectural firms and, 58–59
   environmental design and, 52–53
Digital fluency, 70–71
Dining models, 83–84
Distance learning, 21, 78
Diversity
   demographic changes and, 19–21
   hiring practices and, 44–45
   intersectionality in student affairs, 32–34
   leadership identification and promotion, 43
Donations and gifts, 2–5, 55–56, 108
Drug and alcohol use, 107, 108, 114
Drug-Free Schools and Communities Act (1986), 107
Duke University, Internal Audit Office, 99–100

E

Electronic access to buildings, 89
Emergency allocations, 12–13, 15, 54–55
Emergency preparedness. *See* Crisis response and management
Emotional distress tort claims, 103
Employees. *See also* Human resources
   competencies of. *See* Competencies
   fiduciary risk management and assessment, 13
   food service, 84
   internal communications and, 135–137
   personnel budgets, 6–7
   technology resource allocation and, 72–73
   termination of, 39
   training. *See* Training of staff
   unions for, 7, 84
   workplace assessments by, 136
Enrollment and housing capacity, 54
Enterprise risk management, 98
Equity in pay and other rewards, 34–36
Event management, 5, 82, 86–88
Executive vice president for administration, 25–26
Expense violations, 13
Explicit bias, 43

F

Facilities management, x, 49–67
   athletics facilities, 56, 64, 95
   budget development for capital projects, 8–10
   building access control, 89, 92
   campus master planning and, 50–52
   crisis response plans, 118–119
   environmental design, 52–53
   other student-related facilities, 63–67
   residence hall construction projects, 53–63
   structural failures, 118–119

Faculty
    campus governance models, role in, 24–25
    organizational design and models, role in, 18
Fair Labor Standards Act (1938), 34
Family and Educational Rights and Privacy Act (FERPA, 1974), 20, 75, 106
Federal Sentencing Guidelines, 102
Fees. *See* Student fees
Fiduciary risk assessment and mitigation, 11–14
Financial models for project costs, 55–58
Financing and budgeting, ix–x, 1–16
    alignment of objectives and budgets, 10–11
    best practices, 14–15
    budget breakdown, 3–6
    campus card services and, 92–93
    capital projects, 8–10
    conference and event management, 86–88
    fiduciary risk assessment and mitigation, 11–14
    funding sources, 2–3
    internal audits and, 99
    student affairs budgets, 6–8
Fire, 118–119
Fitness and recreation programs, 93–95
Food services
    data collection and, 90–91
    employees for, 84
    facilities for, 64
    private providers for, 84–86
    student affairs oversight of, 82
    student dining plans, 83–84
Fraud, 13
Funding sources and fundraising
    for auxiliary and other operations, 93–95
    for building projects, 55–56
    fundraising laws, 108
    for institutions, 2–3
    programs for, 4–5
Future of student affairs, x–xi, 78–79, 145–150

G

Gender equity, 106
General counsel's office, 97–98
Generational differences, 33, 70
Gift funds, 2–5, 55–56, 108

H

Healthcare services. *See* Student health centers
Health crises, 119–120
Health Insurance Portability and Accountability Act (HIPAA, 1996), 75, 106
Health records, 75, 106
Higher Education Act (HEA, 1965), 107
Higher Education Reauthorization Act (2019), 20
Hiring practices, 43–45
Human resources, x, 31–48
    equity in pay and other rewards, 34–36
    intersectionality and, 32–34
    leadership identification and promotion, 42–45
    pathways to leadership, 45–46
    performance reviews, 36–37, 38–39
    professional development, 37–42

I

Identification cards, 88–93
Implicit bias, 33, 43
In loco parentis, 20–21
Institutional records, 103–104
Institutional review boards (IRBs), 76, 92
Insurance, 105, 109
Internal audits, 99–100

Internal communications, 135–137
Internal recharges, 3, 5, 87
Intersectionality, 32–34
Investment returns, 2–3

J

Jeanne Clery Disclosure of Campus Security Policy and Campus Crime Statistics Act (1990), 106–107
Job descriptions, 44

L

Lawsuits, 102–106, 109
Leadership and promotion, 42–46
Legal issues and risk management, x, 97–110
  case types and jurisdictions, 102–103
  corporate and enterprise risk management, 98
  depositions, 104–105
  dynamic nature of laws and legal obligations, 108–109
  fiduciary risk assessment and mitigation, 11–14
  general counsel's office, 97–98
  institutional records, 103–104
  internal audits, 99–100
  mediation, settlement, and trial, 105–106
  office of compliance, 100–102
  relevant laws and competencies, 106–108
Liability insurance, 109
Libraries, 90
Local laws, 108

M

Maintenance, 55, 99. *See also* Facilities management
Malfeasance, 28

Media, 117, 141–142
Mediation, 105–106
Medical records, 75, 106
Minorities
  demographic changes and, 19–21
  hiring practices and, 44–45
  intersectionality and, 32–34
  leadership identification and promotion, 43

N

NASPA–Student Affairs Administrators in Higher Education, 39, 70, 148
National Association of Campus Auxiliary Services, 81–82
Negligence, 28, 98, 103
Non-academic services. *See* Auxiliary and other operations

O

Obama, Barack, 106
Office for Civil Rights, 106–107
Office of compliance, 100–102
Organizational design and models, x, 17–29
  campus administrative practices and preferences, 25–27
  campus governance models, 24–25
  demographic changes and expectations of public, 19–21
  design options, 26–27
  faculty role and, 18
  higher education isomorphism, 22–23
  public–private institutional distinctions, 22
  unplanned and unexpected events, influence of, 28–29

P

Parent expectations, 19–21
Parking lots, 89

Parochialism, 22–23, 43
Part-time staff, 34
People with disabilities, 107–108
Performance issues, 43–44
Performance reviews, 36–37, 38–39, 45
Personnel budgets, 7
Philanthropic funding, 2–5, 55–56, 108
Place-making, 51
Police, 118
Prejudice, 43, 44
Preparation and planning for crises, 114–115
Preventative maintenance, 55, 99
Privacy and confidentiality
　academic and research uses of data and, 75–76, 91–92
　communications legal and ethical boundaries, 140–141
　records subpoenas and, 104
　student online spaces and, 71
　student records and data, 74–76, 106
Private food service providers, 84–86
Private institutions, 22, 56, 103–104
Professional development, 37–42
Professional organizations, 39–40, 148
Progress reports, 138
Promotions, 42–46
Proposals for new buildings, 54–55
Protection of data. *See* Data management
Protests, 113, 117–118
Public expectations, 19–21
Public funds, 55, 56
Publicly funded institutions
　capital projects for, 9, 55–58
　institutional records and, 103–104
　state requirements and, 108
　student affairs role in, 22
Public–private partnerships (P3), 10, 57–58
Public safety and health, 118–119

R

Real estate. *See* Facilities management
Records. *See* Data management
Records laws, 103–104, 106
Recreation and fitness programs, 93–95
Renovation projects, 57, 64. *See also* Construction projects
Research data, 75–76, 91–92
Research universities, 18
Reserve accounts, 15, 55–56
Resource allocation and technology, 72–73
Retention notices, 104
Risk management and assessment. *See* Legal issues and risk management
Robotics, 79–80

S

Safety issues, 79, 89, 91, 106–107, 118–119
Salaries, 7, 34–36
Self-assessments, 124
Self-promotion, 45–46
Self-studies, 126–127
Senior administrative officers, 25–26
Services rendered to campus, 3, 5–6, 98
Settlements, 105–106
Sexual misconduct, 103, 106
Smartphones, 73, 88
Social media, 71, 115, 139–140
Sports. *See* Athletics
Staff. *See* Employees; Human resources
State laws, 108
Statewide capital funds, 55, 56
Strategic planning and assessment, x, 121–133
　assessment aspects, 129–130
　benchmarks for, 125–126
　communications and, 137–138
　culture of evidence and, 131–132
　guidelines for, 128

objectives and budgets, alignment of, 10–11
plan execution, 127
point person for, 128
process for, 122–125
regular reviews, 129
self-study, 126–127
Stress tests, 15
Student affairs budgets, 6–8
Student affairs employees. *See* Employees; Human resources
Student clubs and organizations, 21, 75
Student conduct handbooks, 21
Student conduct records, 74–75
Student demographics, 19–21
Student dining plans, 83–84
Student fees, 2, 4, 14, 58, 94
Student health centers, 21, 27, 63–64, 119
Student identification cards, 88–93
Student information databases, 74–75, 106
Student leaders, 115
Student newspapers and reporters, 141–142
Student precincts and neighborhoods, 66–67
Student privacy. *See* Privacy and confidentiality
Student tort claims, 103
Student unions or centers, 26–27, 64–66, 82
Subcontractors, 62
Subpoenas, 104
Survey administration programs, 75–76
SWOT (strengths, weaknesses, opportunities, and threats) analysis, 124

T

Tablets, 73
Teaching universities, 18
Technology, x, 69–80
artificial intelligence and robotics, 79–80
distance learning and, 21, 78
expense violations, avoiding, 13–14
financial implications for, 78
future considerations, 78–79
policies and practices for, 73–75
principles of competencies, 71–72
protection of student data, 75–76
resource allocated for, 72–73
student affairs competencies, 70–71
student identification cards and, 88–93
telehealth services and, 27
third-party partnership and data management, 76–78
Telehealth services, 27
Termination of employees, 39
Third-party partnership and data management, 76–78
Title IX, 103, 106
Tort claims, 103
Training of staff
on budgets, 14
on confidentiality issues, 141
in crisis response and management, 117
professional development and, 37–42
staff development programs, 41–42
technological competencies and, 70–71
Trends and fads, 71
Trials, 105–106
Trump, Donald, 106

U

Unexpected expenses, 11–14
Unions, 7, 84

V

Value engineering, 61
Vice president for student affairs (VPSA), 125, 148

Video communications, 72, 78
Volunteering, 46

W
Webinars, 72

Work–life balance, 35

Z
Zoning laws, 108

Printed in the United States
by Baker & Taylor Publisher Services